Testament
30 Days of Remembrance

DAVID **C** COOK

transforming lives together

This book is dedicated to all my fellow Jesus followers who have their own story of God's radical faithfulness over their lives. These words are some of the personal and glorious testimonies from my own life, the ones that help me remember the robust love of God, especially when walking through fiery trials. I pray they help you remember too.

And they overcame him by the blood of the Lamb
and by the word of their testimony, and they did
not love their lives to the death. (Rev. 12:11 NKJV)

TESTAMENT
Published by David C Cook
4050 Lee Vance Drive
Colorado Springs, CO 80918 U.S.A.

Integrity Music Limited, a Division of David C Cook
Brighton, East Sussex BN1 2RE, England

DAVID C COOK*, the graphic circle C logo and related marks
are registered trademarks of David C Cook.

Bible credits are listed at the back of the book.

Library of Congress Control Number 2024949411
ISBN 978-0-8307-8879-8
eISBN 978-0-8307-8880-4

The Team: Michael Covington, Jeff Gerke, James Hershberger,
Brian Mellema, Jack Campbell, Susan Murdock
Cover Design: Jason Jones, based on *Testament* EP cover design by Pip Ward

Printed in the United States of America
First Edition 2025

1 2 3 4 5 6 7 8 9 10

110724

Acknowledgements

The biggest shout-out here belongs to my hubby, the wonderful Mark Zschech, who *whenever* you see or hear me do anything, you can be guaranteed that he is somewhere close by cheering me on. Thank you, my darling man, not just for loving me, but for really showing me what love looks like.

To my wonderful family (who are my heart wandering outside of my body), your kindness, tenacity, commitment to God and each other, and the way you all love to have *fun* ... I adore you all and can never fully articulate how grateful I am for you.

To Margie Holmes, for being the best PA on the planet for over two decades.

To Zoe Cameron, for entering into our crazy world in a new way—and crushing it!

To Craig Gower, for lending your attention-to-detail skills on my behalf.

To Bev Bekker, for stepping in and bringing your heart and expertise during some tough days.

To the team at David C Cook and all who have worked with me to take this from my heart to these pages.

To our staff and church family at HopeUC ... you are a far greater expression of God's church than we had dared to imagine. Let's keep building and taking the love of Jesus to the world!

I am thankful beyond measure,
With all my heart, Darlene Z

Contents

Visit integritymusic.com/testament or scan the QR code below
to listen to the songs featured in each day of this book!

Introduction

I write this devotional with a heart so filled with love and gratitude for God that, to be honest, putting mere pen to paper seems very limited and analogue. However, God asks us to bring to Him whatever is in our hands ... so here we go.

When I first started on the *Testament* journey, which involves both this devotional and a new album by the same title, it had been many years since I'd spent a long and dedicated period of time in a recording studio. Though the desire had been there, this past season had not really afforded me the months needed to do so. But my family and friends reminded me that "Shout to the Lord" had turned thirty last year (what the what?), and they felt I should do something to mark this moment. So we decided to carve out the time. And with the help of my great and supportive village, *Testament* was birthed.

My son-in-law Andrew suggested the title *Testament*, which can be defined as "a statement of belief or direction" or, in legal terms, "something that serves as evidence of truth; legally binding." Both of those perfectly describe the faithfulness of God, His character and goodness, and every promise contained in the Word of God. I have been re-recording these much-loved songs and writing down my thoughts along the way, which is how this book came to be.

I pray that this journal, these 30 Days of Remembrance, will give you a little insight into these songs of worship. I hope it will help you hear the cry that has been my heart's desire over my lifetime, which is to live in response to the great love of God and *His* unwavering faithfulness over my life.

Really, this is what worship is all about: not platforms for the glory of man, but that the whole of our lives would be poured out for the glory of God. It's not always easy to choose this kind of life, but obedience when following Jesus is the only way you'll ever walk in true freedom. This is my story and the foundation from which *Testament* has been woven together.

> The bedrock of truthful worship is that the
> whole of our lives would be poured out as
> a response to the love of God, enabled by
> the Spirit of God, all for the glory of God

I pray that as you carve out time over this next season to dive into these thoughts, prayers, and stories of God's never-failing love, you will be reminded and encouraged by the rich tapestry of His faithfulness over your own life. This is my deepest prayer for you today.

Listen to "Testament"

Day 1

Testament

How do I even begin to describe the faithfulness of God?

Even on the days that feel impossible or in the long seasons when it seems that winter will never break into spring, there is scripture after scripture about God's faithful nature. Every scribe, writer, and prophet throughout the Word of God communicates this facet of His unending love for His people.

God, You are the author of my days
God, You are the One who makes a way
I'm learning how to trust
When I can't see You clearly
I'm holding onto hope
God, You are the One who'll never change

But mere words will always still fall short of describing how faithful He truly is.

Psalm 89 is a profound psalm of God's faithfulness. It was composed by Ethan the Ezrahite of the tribe of Levi, who wholeheartedly declares what he has found through a life embedded in the Lord.

> I will sing of the LORD's great love forever;
>> with my mouth I will make your faithfulness known
>> through all generations.
> I will declare that your love stands firm forever,
>> that you have established your faithfulness in
>>> heaven itself.
> You said, "I have made a covenant with my chosen one,
>> I have sworn to David my servant,
> I will establish your line forever
>> and make your throne firm through all generations."

> The heavens praise your wonders, LORD,
>> your faithfulness too, in the assembly of the holy ones.
> For who in the skies above can compare with the LORD?
>> Who is like the LORD among the heavenly beings?
> In the council of the holy ones God is greatly feared;
>> he is more awesome than all who surround him.
> Who is like you, LORD God Almighty?
>> You, LORD, are mighty, and your faithfulness
>>> surrounds you. (vv. 1–8)

In Psalm 119:90 the writer continues to testify to the legacy of God's kindness. "Your faithfulness endures to all generations; you have established the earth, and it stands fast."

My personal testimony is that over my lifetime, if I have ever felt like I could not see the Lord, He has always made it clear through His presence and through His written Word that He has never lost sight of me. I was taught as a young Christian to never question God or ask *why* certain things have been part of my story. But as I have matured in my faith, I have found that God has not only invited my questions, but He delights in drawing near to me as I draw near to Him in my wonderings.

I co-wrote the song "Testament" with Andrew (my son-in-love) and Amy (my eldest daughter and Andrew's wife). As we were writing, we wanted to be raw and honest about the pain and suffering in the world (and our world) and the times when what we see or experience may not seem to be lining up with the promises of God.

It's sometimes hard to explain to others our confidence in God's character when life is pushing us to the limits ... but because I know the love of God toward me, I also know He will never abandon or forsake me (Deut. 31:8). When I take the time to listen to Him speak and to notice Him at work even in the smallest of details, and if I will write down the whispers that come in the dry seasons, my heart finds rest and great confidence again that our God Emmanuel is with us. Always.

So today, in whatever place you are starting this journey from, I pray that you will begin with *thanksgiving*. Thank Him, even for all the times you may never know about this side of heaven when God came through and saved you again and again. And for all the times when you have seen His miracle-working power at work in your life, doing the impossible, bringing the miracle light of Christ into the darkest of nights. Also thank Him for all the breakthroughs you are still believing God for. *Hold on!*

The Word of God tells us:

> I have been young, and now am old,
> yet I have not seen the righteous forsaken
> or his children begging for bread. (Ps. 37:25 ESV)

Enter today declaring this over every circumstance in your life. We follow Jesus just as we are today, believing that He will do what He has said He will do, working in and through every circumstance to see His purposes established.

A little reminder: Most times we WILL be required to wait for these miracles to come to pass, but I can guarantee that while we wait, we see so much more of the creativity and nature of God as He shows His faithfulness in different ways along the journey. Learning to wait is one of life's great lessons—and learning to wait *well* is even greater. Learning to trust is what I like to call a superpower, but more on that later.

I pray this stunning Scripture over you today:

> The steadfast love of the LORD never ceases;
> His mercies never come to an end;
> they are new every morning;
> great is your faithfulness. (Lam. 3:22–23 ESV)

Amen and amen. I also love Matthew 11:28: "Come unto me, all who labor and are heavy laden, and I will give you rest" (ESV).

The word *come* in the phrase "come unto me" is from the Greek word *duete,* and it literally means *come*: "come close, come near, come now, I am inviting you to come!" It's the heaven exchange, trading chaos for peace, weakness for strength, heartache for joy. Literally miraculous!

The Greek word behind *labour* is *kopiao*, and it describes a person who has become completely exhausted due to non-stop, continuous work. And here we have Jesus, beckoning every person who feels like this to come to Him and find rest.

He calls not just the hard worker, but also the one who is heavy laden: anyone carrying a very heavy load. And most times, these loads are not physical, but emotional. Emotional heaviness is a critical load. This is the load that weighs our souls down to a place where it can seem to some that their only options are drastic ones.

Years ago my husband, Mark, and I met this very troubled young man on the streets of New York City. He said he could drown out the noise of calamity in his head only by listening to worship, where he would trust that God would trade his own heaviness for God's lightness.

The phrase "give you rest" comes from the Greek word *anapauo*, which means "to refresh or rejuvenate." Without this type of rest that replenishes, our souls become *so* tired. This is when we can find ourselves making foolish or hasty decisions, decisions that will affect many more people than just ourselves.

Learning to rest in God's presence, justice, and God's providence is more "letting go" than "trying hard." It's about learning to release what is in your hand and trust in the character of God.

It's funny that when things feel out of control and we feel overwhelmed, the hardest thing to do in the natural is to *wait* and *trust*. We want to help God out and move things along. Trusting God means trusting in a God you cannot see with the things in your heart that you cannot deal with. Trusting has everything to do with *waiting*.

Being strong in Christ has more to do with sitting than with striving.

Jesus doesn't force Himself into our sphere. He always waits to be welcomed. That's why deliberately leaning into our God is such a worshipful response to Him. It's all about our heart being open toward Him. And in that place of surrender, we hear Him speak, and He fuels us for yet another day.

> Being strong in Christ has more to
> do with sitting than with striving.

Life is all about relationships, and relationships take time. And *time* is the most precious commodity we have on earth. So even though you may think you have no time to just wait on God, it's actually in the waiting that you'll find strategy, answers, resolve, and peace for the journey.

Some questions for you to think on today.

How do you respond when you are being unjustly treated?

What do you do when you feel you have no obvious way forward?

What do you do when you know, deep down, that somehow the promises of God will prevail, but today, they seem so far away from your reality?

Listen to "Shout to the Lord"

Day 2

Nothing Compares
(Shout to the Lord)

When I look back at that very precious season of my life when "Shout to the Lord" was written, I recall that though it was a season that required me to dig very deep wells in God, it was also full of the best things in life. And digging Jesus wells is always *so* wonderful in the end, as they take time and intentionality.

Back then, our girls were just little and playful and filled with wonder. Since being a wife and mum was and is my greatest dream, these were days I treasure with my whole heart. In many ways, the busy season of parenting young kids forces you into a simplicity and a rhythm that brings so much joy to life (even when you are feeling exhausted!).

The day I wrote "Shout to the Lord," as I sat at my very old and out-of-tune piano in a tiny little hallway of our home, even though circumstances in our lives at that point were less than ideal, with my two precious daughters running and playing around me, the presence and kindness of God met me in that glorious moment. The lyric "Nothing compares to the promise I have in you" is still the line that gets me undone, as it is as true today as it was back then.

If I am super honest, I am not great at speaking well "in the moment." I always need time and space to gather my thoughts into ways that make sense to the listener. And writing has always given me a way to at least *try* to give voice to things that rumble around inside my heart and mind. And that was the gift of that day: setting time aside to pour out my heart before God, and Him meeting me with His presence. I literally just sat playing and worshipping and singing out the Psalms and God's promises over our lives.

Shout to the Lord
All the earth let us sing
Power and majesty
Praise to the King
Mountains bow down
And the seas will roar
At the sound of Your name
I sing for joy at the work of Your hands
Forever I'll love You, forever I'll stand
Nothing compares to the promise
I have in You

How do you go with believing God's promises over your life?

Every year, Mark and I try to pull out every prophetic word that has been spoken over us, our girls, our family, and our church. And yes, it is a lot, but what it does within us is help us remember God's mighty voice and promises over our lives. We also do a little "stock take" to see if there are areas where we are maybe a little out of alignment with where we feel God is leading us. Maybe this is something you can begin in your life. *You are worth it.*

"Nothing compares to the promise I
have in you" still gets me undone, as it
is as true today as it was back then.

I have many journals filled with Scripture, promises, notes, and reminders. Being a Christian for over forty years and following a speaking God, there has been *a lot* to listen to. Sometimes I have to discipline myself to get off YouTube and Insta so I can fill my heart and head with the things the Lord has already spoken to my heart. I must choose to welcome His Word to shape me, rejecting the opinions or experiences of others who try to tell me where I am going or who I am.

When I meditate on Scriptures like 1 Corinthians 2, my heart feels like it wants to explode, knowing that the God of all creation actually has prepared to include us in His glorious plans.

As it is written:

> What no eye has seen, what no ear has heard,
>   and what no human mind has conceived
> The things God has prepared for those who love him
>   These are the things God has revealed to us by his
>   Spirit.
> The Spirit searches all things, even the deep things of
>   God. (vv. 9–10)

I have been challenged many times by the writings of John Wesley. When writing on following Jesus with his whole life and while holding on to every scripture, he said this:

> I am no longer my own, but Yours. Put me to what You will, rank me with whom You will; put me to doing, put me to suffering; let me be employed for You or laid aside for You, exalted for You or brought low for You; let me be full, let me be empty; let me have all things, let me have nothing; I freely and wholeheartedly yield all things to Your pleasure and disposal.[1]

This puts everything into perspective. The testimony of God's incomparable love toward us means that we decide daily to follow Him no matter what. Sadly, sometimes we interpret the promises of God in ways that are a little more Disney than Bible.

An incredible example of this is the story of Stephen in Acts 6. Stephen is the first Christian martyr in the Bible, the first person we know of who dies for his faith in Jesus.

> As the believers rapidly multiplied, there were rumblings of discontent. The Greek-speaking believers complained about the Hebrew-speaking believers, saying that their widows were being discriminated against in the daily distribution of food.
>
> So the Twelve called a meeting of all the believers. They said, "We apostles should spend our time teaching the word of God, not running a food program. And so, brothers, select seven men who are well respected and are full of the Spirit and wisdom. We will give them this responsibility. Then we apostles can spend our time in prayer and teaching the word."
>
> Everyone liked this idea, and they chose the following: Stephen (a man full of faith and the Holy Spirit), Philip, Procorus, Nicanor, Timon, Parmenas, and Nicolas of Antioch. These seven were presented to the apostles, who prayed for them as they laid their hands on them. (vv. 1–6 NLT)

I believe Stephen was chosen for this task for many reasons. First, he and the other six were men of good reputation. Second, he was full of the Spirit. He was already following Jesus in a way that revealed God's presence and power. Third, the passage says he and the others were full of wisdom. With the expanding influence of this young and growing church, wisdom was needed.

Finally, Stephen is described as a man full of faith.

That's three "fulls": Spirit, wisdom and faith.

He was walking the Christian life at a level that we would think set him up to be like the apostles, and yet this is a man who was asked to wait tables. He could have refused, but he did not see this role as beneath him or out of alignment with God's purpose over his life. This was a man captivated by the truth that "nothing compares to the promise" he had in Jesus.

Stephen wasn't waiting on tables for long. The same chapter of Acts tells us how certain Jewish religious leaders turned on him and brought him before their court to answer for his actions. That court assembly turned into a violent mob, and they stoned Stephen to death.

A reader might think this remarkable man's story ends right there, but it didn't. As Stephen followed Jesus to glory, a certain man stood by looking on. The apostle Paul (then called Saul) stood among the mob and witnessed something that would shape his life forever.

Can we trust God's plans?
Can we trust His promises?
Even if what we experience feels nothing like
how we thought God would answer us?

If we truly can trust Him, then we can yield to His will, and that is where the glory of God's promises begins to unfold.

Day 3

Shout It Out

"In Jesus' Name" is a song I wrote in 2012 with my friend Israel Houghton. It was a season where my girlfriends and I at church were walking with a beautiful woman named Deb as she battled a long and hard road with cancer. We prayed with her, we sang with her, we danced with her, we took communion with her, and yet finally she went home to be with Jesus, and her soul and flesh were finally at rest.

At the same time, we were walking through other tough cancer journeys with family members, and I just remember going into the studio and shouting, "I hate cancer!" Israel and I ended up writing this song fairly quickly, especially the bridge:

> *God is fighting for us, pushing back the darkness*
> *Lighting up the Kingdom that cannot be shaken*
> *In the Name of Jesus, enemies defeated*
> *And we will shout it out, shout it out*

We sang it and declared it. It became a song of hope for many others. People wrote to us saying how they literally clung to the declaration as they walked through terror-filled seasons.

It was December 13, 2013, when I received a very shocking breast cancer diagnosis of my own. Only a week later, on December 20, 2013, I went into hospital for surgery. I got home to begin recovery on Christmas Eve, and I began prepping my body for 2014, which would be a year of treatment.

This was the most fear-filled thing I have ever walked through. If it hadn't have been for my family and friends and the life-giving presence of God, I just don't know how I would have journeyed through. My soul was really battling. I have stood and sung and prayed over so many fighting this sickness, how on earth could this happen to me?

During this time, I continued to lead worship when I had the energy. To be honest, it helped me just to make the Word of God louder than the fear and doubt rolling around in my head. But I noticed that over time I had stopped *shouting it out*. In worship I had begun to retreat to places that required little faith, as I was nervous to raise my voice to align my life to the truth of God's Word. Evil had silenced me. The day I realised this, I was really shocked at how intimidated by the enemy I had become.

If we truly can trust Him, then we can
yield to His will, and that is where the
glory of God's promises begins to unfold.

Mark and I ended up spending some time with Pastor Bill Johnson from Bethel Church in Redding, who was visiting from America at a church only an hour away from our home. He was gracious enough to take some time to sit with us. He just let us talk out our fears and concerns, all the while he lovingly listened like a good father would. In the end, he encouraged us, prayed with us, hugged us, and without any judgement, said it was time to lift my voice again. He said I had to start *pushing back* with the Word of God. He said there would be a day when I would find my strength and internal roar again.

We went home feeling like we had courage once more. We were ready to say *no* to the enemy's plans over our lives.

Exodus 14:13 says, "Moses answered the people, 'Do not be afraid. Stand firm and you will see the deliverance the LORD will bring you today. The Egyptians you see today you will never see again.'"

Stand firm. Do not be afraid.

I began to see that for me to step over fear and stand in truth, I had to find ways to yield the things that were trying to limit my expression of faith. I needed to fall on my knees and surrender to the plans that God was working together in my life for my good and His glory.

There are times in your life when silence and solitude are a necessary partner to your followship of Jesus, to turn down the noise of this world and sit in the nearness of God. But there are also times when a prophetic *shout* is needed to tell the atmosphere around you how it needs to respond when you are present. My friend Alicia Britt Chole says, "A shout doesn't thicken who God is, just as a whisper does not diminish who God is,"[2] but there are times when one or the other is needed.

When I first started leading worship, I felt quite inhibited when it came to shouting praise to God or even expressing my worship in genuine freedom. I guess being so dedicated to not drawing attention to myself caused my insecurities to dictate what expression was okay for me to participate in. It wasn't until the revelation of God's worth and weight grew inside of me that my inhibitions began to crumble. God's Word showed me that my response to His great love would never be found in a textbook but would come out of my inner being as I welcomed His love to heal me and fuel my faith, even as I led others in worship. There was something about stepping over the fear that started to rebuild a spiritual tenacity.

In this and every season of my life, I have had to dig deep and re-engage with what I know to be true. The shout of faith often carries the seeds of prophetic insight, as we loudly verbalize what we see in the spiritual, regardless of circumstance or prevailing emotional strongholds.

My encouragement to you today is this: There may be situations in your life where you too have sat down and gone quiet in the pain. There was a time when Esther had to speak up. There was a time when Moses had to get over his own inadequacies and speak out. Maybe it's time for you to stand again and speak out the truth of God's Word over your life.

Trust in God! Shout His goodness. Rest in His kindness. There are beautiful days ahead filled with the miraculous as we just take obedient steps one at a time.

Listen to "Victor's Crown."

Day 4

Victor's Crown

It's so interesting to me that I sometimes receive pushback over this song. "Victor's Crown" really helped me find my anchor in a crazy and dark storm, and it helped many others do the same.

My husband often says, "Never waste a good crisis," and he's right. Our family has had our fair share of crisis days—and crisis *seasons*—and I am sure yours has too. As Christians, what these seasons really do is ask you to sort out your theology on pain and suffering. They cause you to find out what you believe about where Jesus is in the midst of it all.

When I was a young Christian, I often felt like we weren't allowed to tell anyone about hard times. The implication was that if you found a certain situation painful or difficult, it meant you had no faith. I remember thinking, *Isn't crying out for help the whole point? Isn't His grace made perfect in my weakness?* But I digress.

The first lines of this song go like this:

You are always fighting for us
Heaven's angels all around
My delight is found in knowing
That You wear the Victor's crown
You're my help and my defender
You're my Savior and my friend
By Your grace I live and breathe to worship You

Those thoughts came from Deuteronomy 3:22: "Do not be afraid of them; the LORD your God himself will fight for you." When you feel you have no fight left, what do you do? He is always fighting for us. Over the course of many years, I have learned how to fall into the hands of my loving and caring Saviour.

When I wrote that my delight is found in knowing that He wears the Victor's Crown, I was thinking about the crown originally forced on Jesus' head—the crown of thorns, which was intended as a crown of ridicule and pain. When Jesus said, "It is finished" (John 19:30), He became the ultimate victor, and that is where the words *Victor's Crown* come from. In Hebrews 2:9 it says, "But we see Jesus ... crowned with glory and honour; that he by the grace of God should taste death for every man" (KJV).

Death could not hold Jesus down. Resurrection life was on the way, preparing the greatest triumph in history—and for eternity, for the final victory will always belong to the Lord.

When I apply this understanding to our momentary trials, I find that now my faith has a job to do: to stand on the Scriptures and trust God to do what He said He would do.

> Consider it pure joy, my brothers and sisters, whenever you face trials of many kinds, because you know that the testing of your faith produces perseverance. Let perseverance finish its work so that you may be mature and complete, not lacking anything. (James 1:2–4)

The resurrection fuels my hope. And the words of Christ feed my faith, especially when what I read and what I am experiencing don't seem to line up. This is where our confidence comes in, really knowing that our God is the ultimate victor.

There is a bridge section of this song that again builds my faith:

> *Every high thing must come down*
> *Every stronghold shall be broken*
> *You wear the Victor's crown*
> *You overcome, You overcome*

These words are accompanied by a rhythm that feels a little like warfare. A warrior mindset is where I often go in leading worship. I declare the promises of God and lead others in their confessions of faith.

Listen to this, my friend: "Our struggle is not against flesh and blood, but against the rulers, against the authorities, against the powers of this dark world and against the spiritual forces of evil in the heavenly realms" (Eph. 6:12).

This is where our battle cry comes from: standing on the Word and declaring that Jesus has overcome it all!

> I find that now my faith has a job to do: to stand on the Scriptures and trust God to do what He said He would do.

And beyond warfare terminology, the Bible also encourages us to run our race, to not look back, to not compare, and to run for a crown that will last forever.

"Everyone who competes in the games goes into strict training. They do it to get a crown that will not last, but we do it to get a crown that will last forever" (1 Cor. 9:25).

This crown is called an "imperishable crown" in 1 Peter 1:4. In fact, there are quite a few crowns listed in the Word of God that talk about God's children receiving their crowns at the end of their lives or the end of time as we know it. There's the crown of rejoicing in 1 Thessalonians 2:19, the crown of righteousness in 2 Timothy 4:8, and the crown of life in Revelation 2:10, amongst others.

All I know is that when we see Jesus face to face, we won't be thinking about which crowns we are going to receive. Maybe we will just fall on our knees in worship of the One who has won it all. We will find ourselves in a place of reverential awe and worshipful surrender.

> They lay their crowns before the throne and say:
>   "You are worthy, our Lord and God,
>   to receive glory and honor and power,
>   for you created all things
>   and by your will they were created
>   and have their being." (Rev. 4:10–11)

A question for you today:

What crowns do you maybe need to lay down?

The crowns of self-righteousness and opinion are ones we should readily lay aside. Some of the others are a little harder to see that we are wearing, such as the crown of unknown bias or racism, or the crown of being a self-made person not needful of anyone or anything else. I am sure that you, like me, can write your own list.

In the end, I take any crown I've ever worn, and I lay it down. Then I crown my Jesus with many crowns—with every crown. With my life, with my worship, with my all.

Day 5

Potter's Hand

Yet you, LORD, are our Father.
We are the clay, you are the potter;
We are all the work of your hand. (Isa. 64:8)

Have you ever watched an artisan who really knows how to use a potter's wheel? I love how they take clay and a little bit of water and turn something very plain into something very beautiful. It is captivating to watch, and they make it look so effortless.

Once, inspired to try something new, I did a pottery class with my sister. And yes, it was SO much fun! But the pottery pieces I imagined I would be making were not quite the pieces that my unskilled hands ended up creating. It was much harder than I thought it would be. When we finally felt we had done our best and took our pieces to the kiln, we all had a little laugh at these lopsided vases. The teacher praised our efforts, but maybe with a slight grin on her face.

The beautiful thing about clay is that no matter how misshapen a clump has become, it can be "thrown" down and the moulding can begin again. That's a picture of our lives too, as described here in Isaiah 64. We are the clay, God is the master craftsman, and we are the work of His hand.

> This is the word that came to Jeremiah from the LORD: "Go down to the potter's house, and there I will give you my message." So I went down to the potter's house, and I saw him working at the wheel. But the pot he was shaping from the clay was marred in his hands; so the potter formed it into another pot, shaping it as seemed best to him. (Jer. 18:1–4)

In Jeremiah 18, we find Jeremiah exhausted in his efforts to turn the heart of Israel back to God. And God shows him something in the natural: a revolving wheel, a lump of clay, water, and the potter. Then He relates it to Jeremiah's problem, showing that only if the nation is willing to go back and submit to the master potter's hand will there be any hope for Israel.

God is always working at His wheel, but the fact is that we can either resist the potter or work with the potter. There is no neutral or middle ground. Yielding our will and our way, our plans and our opinions, and welcoming the person of the Holy Spirit to lead us is the only way to become more like Jesus. If you read on in this chapter of Jeremiah, you will see that the jar God was making did not turn out as He hoped. It was failing to respond to the potter's hand. And so He just grabbed the clay and put it back on the wheel ... and started again.

Ouch. Have you ever felt like you've been put back on the wheel?

At some point in our Christian walk, we have to learn to trust the Master Potter. Because clay without the potter's touch just remains as mud.

I love the thought that in God's master plan for our lives, there are no mass-produced products, no throwaway expendable cups, just once-in-a-lifetime, designed-for-a-purpose, wonderfully made creations. That's who each of us is. Sometimes it's hard to see the beauty ourselves, as we may only see the flaws, the shortcomings, the things yet to be perfected.

For clay to yield to the Master's touch, He needs to bring pressure to it, and the clay needs more water. In the Bible, the symbol of water is often used to describe the work of the Holy Spirit. And just like water is essential for physical wholeness, so the water of God's Spirit is essential for spiritual wholeness. And the pressure, well, that helps us to be shaped in the right direction.

And I would love to say that then the work is done. But no ... there's more. The Master Potter pops that glorious piece of artwork into the *fire*. For without the fire, there is no lasting pottery. Without the work of the heat, the clay might dry and look somewhat right, but it would only disintegrate under the first moment of pressure. Hmm.

Hebrews 12:28–29 says, "Therefore, since we are receiving a kingdom that cannot be shaken, let us be thankful, and so worship God acceptably with reverence and awe, for our 'God is a consuming fire.'"

> At some point, we have to learn to trust the Master Potter. Because clay without the potter's touch just remains as mud.

There is something very powerful here. The writer is reminding us that the kingdom of God is unlike any other earthly kingdom, all of which can and will give way eventually. He reminds us that in the shaking, we are to remain thankful and worship God. It's in the safety of God's presence that our hearts will remain soft and pliable while we are on the wheel.

Verse 29 describes God as a consuming, cleansing refiner's fire. Resilience is formed in the fire. Finding out what you believe happens in the fire. It's essential too to discover that you are still safe in the fire even as you are fashioned toward God's heart for you. There is great relief in understanding the purpose and the process of the fire.

Charles Spurgeon said:

Everything that is holy will endure the fire, and as for all within us that is impure, let it be consumed speedily. So let us serve the Lord with fear, but not with terror, and let this service be continued all our days.[3]

The consuming fire is all about becoming more like Jesus even as our flesh wrestles against the remaking. We are safe in the hands of the Master Potter.

Are there any areas of your life today that you feel like you are on the Potter's wheel?

My prayer over our lives today:

> *Take me, mold me*
> *Use me, fill me*
> *I give my life to the Potter's hands*
> *Hold me, guide me*
> *Lead me, walk beside me*
> *I give my life to the Potter's hand*

Listen to "Daylight"

Day 6

Daylight

You, LORD, are the Most High over all the earth;
you are exalted far above all gods. (Ps. 97:9)

The writer in me loves those days when a friend comes to help me declare and write down the musings of my heart. The song "Daylight" came about just like that. This precious friend, Beth Gleeson, sat with me at the piano, and after a little while, our hearts collided in all the best possible ways. With Psalm 97 guiding the thought process, two hearts overflowed with thankfulness and filled in the gaps.

We were both talking about the beauty of God's mercy, how His mercies are new every morning, how daylight breaks over us all ... and that there is *nothing* that can separate us from His love. *No thing.*

While I was writing this chapter, I felt led to take a minute to make an important point: There is not one ounce of God's nature that tries to minimise or put a lid on those of us who are female. No, being female has never separated us from God's love or made us "slightly less than" our male brothers. God Himself has never put restrictions on my passion to serve Him, disqualified me from rising up to lead others in the songs of God, or (dare I even say it?), sharing the good news of the gospel with others.

God has been using women to bring glory to His name since the beginning of time. Interestingly, the first worship leader mentioned in the Bible was Moses' sister, Miriam, who praised God on her tambourine after Pharaoh and his army were drowned in the Red Sea (see Ex. 15:20–21).

Both Deborah (Judges 5) and Hannah (1 Samuel 2) are recorded as singing songs of praise. God has never restricted women in their leadership or worship; He has only encouraged it (for *all* of us) as a rightful response to His worth.

In Luke 7, we read of this precious worshipper—unnamed to us, but deeply known to Jesus:

> When one of the Pharisees invited Jesus to have dinner with him, he went to the Pharisee's house and reclined at the table. A woman in that town who lived a sinful life learned that Jesus was eating at the Pharisee's house, so she came there with an alabaster jar of perfume. As she stood behind Him at His feet weeping, she began to wet His feet with her tears. Then she wiped them with her hair, kissed them and poured perfume on them.

When the Pharisee who had invited him saw
this, he said to himself, "If this man were a prophet,
he would know who is touching him and what kind
of woman she is—that she is a sinner. (vv. 36–39)

This woman (who in some translations of the Bible is called "an
especially wicked sinner") boldly came to Jesus while He was dining
with Simon the Pharisee. (Don't you love that Jesus eats with everyone?)

Her actions must have seemed scandalous. First, because of how
women were viewed in that time, and second, because of her reputation. Yet Jesus' *mercy* was (and is) so wonderful that her response to
His love caused her to express her thankfulness to Him, completely
defying the protocols of the day. This is worship.

Jesus ... His mercy and love, so far-reaching, can never be
exhausted. His kindness is always drawing us to Himself. It's interesting to me that people often judge others' worship through their own
filters, quickly disqualifying expressions, offerings, or even lyrics that
may exceed their own ability to express exuberant thanksgiving to
God. Over the years, I have had people say they would not sing some
of my songs because the lyrics are too personal and should never have
been sung in a public space.

But the fact is that when we receive the great saving love of God,
our response is always pure, uninhibited worship. It may be in song, it
may be in service, it may be in loving the wounded, it may be in any
measure of sacrifice, but it will always produce a response. It does not

need to be wildly demonstrative, but God does require from you whatever is genuine. Gentle heartfelt whispers uttered in truth are glorious, as are exuberant and loud declarations of "worthship."

Fanny Crosby, the famous hymn writer from the 1800s, was constantly criticised for being outlandish and emotional in her hymn writing. Though her title even at the time was "the mother of congregational singing in America," and though it was said that she wrote more than nine thousand hymns, it was also said that she had to use over two hundred pseudonyms during her lifetime. Why? Because many people would not have sung her songs had they known a woman had written them.

This attitude toward women has changed over the years in some places, but not in many parts of the world. That deeply saddens me. I am so grateful that, thanks to my parents and my church leaders over the years, I have never been made to feel like anything is out of reach for me because I am female. Maybe for other reasons, but never due to my gender.

If it is in your power to do so, make sure you are in an environment that champions God's call on your life, whoever you are and whatever it is. And if this is not possible for you, pray that a door opens to find yourself elsewhere. You are worth it. Our God is a waymaker—this I know to be true. Making ways in seemingly impossible situations is actually His character.

Back to our story of this woman's extravagant act of love with the expensive perfume. Worship, when genuine, will always lead to a deeper revelation of Jesus. Sometimes, perhaps oftentimes, it will be misunderstood. And that's okay.

Life can be scary, frustrating, uncertain, yet resting in the presence of Jesus and fixing your gaze on Him will not only put all things into perspective but will bring you into a glorious peace that really does pass all understanding. Freedom is a powerful thing.

> Our God is a waymaker. Making ways in seemingly impossible situations is actually His character.

Our God truly is God most high, who hears every cry and who comes to our defence. He is the only one worthy of all our adoration and praise. What a beautiful time it was that day with my friend Beth as we prayed, wrote, and sang glory to our God, with no restriction or even a pressure to write anything that anyone else would listen to. This is SO freeing.

Are the environments you are in conducive to calling out God's best for you? Are you also calling out God's best in those around you?

Daylight

I will dwell in Your promise
In the light of Your truth
You're the Hope that sustains me
Always safe here with You
You are here in the valley

You are here in the storm
You're the glory of daylight
Breaking through like the dawn

And You are God Most High
Yet You hear my cry
And You run to my defence
And I will walk unharmed
Angels all around
I will trust and not be moved

In Your love I'm protected
I will stand and I will sing
You're the God of angel armies
Heaven's wings over me
You're the God of angel armies
Heaven's wings over me

You won't let go
You won't give in
You surround me with Your love
Your majesty it covers me
You surround me with Your love

By Darlene Zschech and Beth Gleeson

Listen to "Soli Deo Gloria."

Day 7

Soli Deo Gloria

I thought about this theme for years before this song came to be. It wasn't until I was sitting in a writing room with our dear friends Dustin Smith and Mitch Wong that the idea met their brilliance and the song was born.

I am captivated by the life story of Johann Sebastian Bach (1685–1750). I *love* this quote from him: "The aim and final end of all music should be none other than the glory of God and the refreshment of the soul." Bach lived his life in this pursuit, inspired by 1 Corinthians 10:31: "Whatever you eat or drink, or whatever you do, do it all for the glory of God." At the end of many of Bach's compositions, you will find the initials S.D.G. This is short for *Soli Deo Gloria*, which means "To God alone, the glory."

When David wanted to give us a picture of God's glory, he asked us to look at the heavens, as they "declare the glory of God" (Ps. 19:1).

So many attributes of God are on display in the heavens: His beauty, His majesty, His holiness, His creativity. I don't know which ones David had in mind. But what I do know for sure is that you cannot miss the glory of God. You may call it something else. It may be something that renders you speechless with magnificence. Maybe it's something that leaves you in awe, understanding your small place in the grand scheme of things. I have heard it described as the *otherness* of God. But when His glory is revealed to you and in you, your life begins to be changed by the weight and worth of His brilliance.

The Bible also tells us that *all* glory belongs to the Lord. For example: "Grow in the grace and knowledge of our Lord and Savior Jesus Christ. To him be the glory both now and to the day of eternity. Amen" (2 Pet. 3:18 ESV).

When we experience the glory of God, there is nothing quite like it. And giving God all the glory *is* our rightful response to His wonder and worth.

But there are times when we see the glory of God trying to be claimed by humanity. This is where the weakness of humanity can cause us to come undone. Romans 1:25 says, "They exchanged the truth about God for a lie, and worshiped and served created things rather than the Creator—who is forever praised. Amen."

> When God's glory is revealed, your
> life begins to be changed by the
> weight and worth of His brilliance.

I feel like we all wrestle with what I would call "glory wars." We were created to carry glory, reflect glory, and give all glory to God, but *not* to receive it ourselves. We are not built for it. How many times have we witnessed amazing people being literally ruined by believing they were the main contributor to the greatness on their lives? We can so quickly tip into performance mode, which is followed by striving, and then we try to sustain in the flesh what began in the Spirit. This is something we all need to be aware of. We *should* do great things, but as Bach modelled for us, they must be for the glory of God alone.

It was an exciting few hours in the studio as we worked on this song.

Actually, we could have written many songs about God's infinite glory that day. We were so inspired by the majesty of God, and when you start talking with other Christian creatives about this topic, it helps unlock new narratives as you bounce ideas off one another. I believe that God has created each of us in ways that help show a different colour of God's magnificence, and we can and should be proud of our work. But staying grateful for the gifts God has given us is a great way to protect our hearts from receiving what is only ours to give.

Is it possible to stay in that posture of humility? In any walk of life, we can bring our talents, skills, energy, and focus to our tasks, and this often brings with it a measure of applause from man. So how can we avoid the pride trap?

I love David's revelation in Psalm 92:

You oh Lord, are exalted forever
   in the highest place of endless glory
While all your opponents, the workers of wickedness,
      they will all perish, forever separated from You
Your anointing has made me strong and mighty.
      You've empowered my life for triumph
You've said that those lying in wait to pounce on
      me would be defeated And now it's happened
      right in front of my eyes.
And I've heard their cries of surrender
Yes! Look how You've made all your lovers to flourish
      like palm trees, each one growing in victory,
      standing with strength!
You've transplanted them into your heavenly
      courtyard where they are thriving before You.
For in Your presence they will still overflow and
      be anointed. Even in their old age they will
      stay fresh, bearing luscious fruit and abiding
      faithful.
Listen to them! with pleasure they still proclaim:
      You're so good! You're my beautiful strength!
      You've never made a mistake with me.
      (vv. 8–15 TPT)

Twice in here he talks about being anointed.

In the King James Bible, Psalm 92:10b is rendered, "I shall be anointed with fresh oil."

I won't get into a deep teaching on anointing oil, but I will talk about the importance of being anointed with fresh oil daily.

I remember one of my children's school projects when they were young. The class was learning about the wonder of a duck (remember these projects?). Ducks have a special gland near their tails called the preen gland. This gland produces an oil that ducks rub over their feathers with their beaks to maintain their waterproof effect. This oil creates a protective barrier that prevents feathers from becoming waterlogged. The action a duck uses to apply this oil is called *preening*.

In the Old Testament, shepherds used a similar method. They would pour oil on a sheep's head to keep it free of lice and other insects that would easily kill the sheep. Put that oil on, and the little critters would just slide off! This was called *anointing* the sheep. This word became symbolic of blessing, favour, protection, and empowerment.

The anointing on our lives is not there to impress others—it is there to reveal God's glory. It is there to keep our lives "oily" so that all the things that could harm us have to slide right off.

This is also why being part of a community or family of faith is so important. When we isolate ourselves from true community, we become like vulnerable prey, believing our own good (or bad) press, and allowing the wrong things to stick to us.

How do you go with receiving praise? Or even criticism?

Is this a healthy part of your soul or maybe a part that needs some attention?

May we be more like Mr. Bach. May over every day of our lives it be written S.D.G.

Soli Deo Gloria

We come before Your throne
to worship and adore
worthy is the Lamb
Amen

Robed in majesty
our Servant and our King
Behold the Great I am
Amen

The hope of every heart
Love is here with us
Desire of the nations
Amen

All that is bows down
All that breathes cries out
At the mention of your name
Earth and heaven shout
Praise that shakes the ground
For the glory of Your name
Jesus Jesus

Day 8

His Glory Appears

Arise, Jerusalem! Let your light shine for all to see.
For the glory of the LORD rises to shine on you.
Darkness as black as night covers all the nations of
    the earth,
but the glory of the Lord rises and appears over you.
All nations will come to your light;
mighty kings will come to see your radiance.
        (Isa. 60:1–3 NLT)

I love this chapter of the Bible for many reasons. I love its command to rise—not in our own light or strength but because the glory of the living God has risen upon us.

Let's continue to look at the word *glory*, as there is just *so* much to unpack.

When I prayed to commit my life to Jesus, repent of my sin, and ask the Lord to fill me with His Spirit, I didn't know what it all meant ... but my heart had never felt so sure about anything. It was as if my soul was sensing the reality of a world or a way that could possibly bring relief to my brokenness. I was being interrupted by *glory*, which in this case I might define as the weight of God's love for me.

So there I was now spiritually joined to Him who deserves all glory and dominion forever (which we spoke about in the previous chapter), and something like a wildfire started to take hold of me for my life's purpose.

> Since the creation of the world God's invisible qualities—His eternal power and divine nature— have been clearly seen, being understood from what has been made, so that people are without excuse. (Rom. 1:20)

My friend, since the creation of the world, God's very nature and qualities have been revealed to the hearts of men and woman like you and me. He has made it possible for us to exchange our present darkness for His presence and light.

The presence of God—His nearness and very being—made evident in our midst is just a part of the wonder of the glory of God.

> Then Moses said, "Now show me your glory."
> And the LORD said, "I will cause all my goodness to pass in front of you, and I will proclaim my name,

the LORD, in your presence. I will have mercy on
whom I will have mercy, and I will have compassion
on whom I will have compassion." (Ex. 33:18–19)

The Hebrew word for *glory* used by Moses was *kabowd*. It is
defined by Strong's Bible Dictionary as "the weight of something, but
only figuratively in a good sense." Its definition also speaks of splendour, abundance, and honour.

Scholars struggle to find adequate words to define God's glory.
Moses was asking, "Show me Yourself in all Your splendour." Look
carefully at God's response: "I will make all My goodness pass before
you, and I will proclaim the name of the LORD before you" (Ex.
33:19 NKJV).

Moses requested all His glory, and God referred to it as "all My
goodness." The Hebrew word for *goodness* is *tuwb*. It means, "good in
the widest sense." In other words, a situation in which nothing good
is withheld.

Then God says, "I will proclaim the name of the LORD before
you."

We see then that the glory of the Lord is everything that makes
God, God. It's the fullness of His nature wrapped in the power of His
name. It's the expanse of God's being. I think this is part of the reason
God created us with the capability of creative expression. Every person
who has ever lived and ever will live can use whatever they have and
are to give glory to God through every aspect of their lives. We can

creatively glorify God as we write, sing, plan, create, build, pray, care, teach, cook, parent … the creative list goes on and on. Even by doing such things over a lifetime, we cannot adequately tell the story of the wonder and glory of our God. It blows my mind.

His Glory Appears

You gave me hope
You made me whole
At the cross

You took my place
You showed me grace
At the cross where You died for me

And His glory appears
Like the light from the sun
Age to age He shines
Oh, look to the skies
Hear the angels cry
Singing holy is the Lord

"His Glory Appears" was written to communicate the intersection between the wandering human heart and the kindness of God. The cross of Christ is the ultimate nexus where earth and heaven meet.

The glory of the Lord is everything that makes God, God.

How would I explain what glory feels like? I might say it's like a deep breath of relief. Or a gift that continues to reveal layers of God's goodness. The gentle breeze on a hellishly hot day? A warmth in my innermost being that whispers hope to me? Perhaps it's what we feel when we watch God move in people's lives as we worship Him. Seeing and experiencing transformation, beauty for ashes, the oil of joy for mourning as the glory of God is made visible amongst us?

I recently sat in the NICU with a family who were passing back to God their child who had tragically passed away. I sensed God's tangible presence and kindness. He came in very close and wrapped the heartbroken family in His layers of "Godness" (I know that's not a word, but I don't know how else to explain the moment!). I witnessed glory in motion as they wept and praised, with all their questions and grief, yet God never turned away. If anything, He just seemed larger.

If you have experienced the glory of God in a tangible way, can you explain what it was like? Most times it's hard to put into words, but it's good to try.

"We all, with unveiled face, beholding the glory of the Lord, are being transformed into the same image from one degree of glory to another. For this comes from the Lord who is the Spirit" (2 Cor. 3:18 ESV).

Another beautiful part of God's glory is in our becoming more like Jesus. My identity is not found in being applauded or accepted by others, but by being found in Christ. His glory is seen through a life yielded to the Spirit of God. We don't seek glory; we just seek Jesus. And His glory, stunningly, is part of that overflow that is revealed and seen in us.

We see the actual word "glory" used in the Bible in over six hundred places, and you cannot translate it easily, whether in Hebrew, Greek, or Aramaic. It has a great depth of meaning. It can mean worth or intricate value. It can mean God's supreme greatness. Its meaning encompasses how our lives are changed by Jesus. It means dignity, majesty and honour. It's even used when the Bible is explaining heaven.

His glory appears again and again whenever the greatness of God interrupts our human existence.

You are a carrier of God's glory and a reflection of God's glory. Since this is so, how does this affect the way you live? It truly will have an impact on the entirety of your life. Take a moment to reflect on this thought.

Let me leave you with a portion from another precious psalm of David declaring God's wondrous glory:

You, God, are my God,
  earnestly I seek you;
  I thirst for you,
  my whole being longs for you,
  in a dry and parched land
  where there is no water.
  I have seen you in the sanctuary
  and beheld your power and your glory.
  Because your love is better than life,
  my lips will glorify you. (Ps. 63:1–3)

Listen to "At the Cross."

Day 9

At the Cross

A magnificent elderly gentleman in our church said something wonderful one day as we gathered around communion. He said, "Prayer is us toward God; communion is God toward us." I have pondered and treasured this statement deeply in my heart, and ever since I have received the gift of communion more intentionally maybe than ever before.

When I was walking through chemotherapy treatment, God gave me the most amazing revelation about the power of the cross and how Jesus actually paid the price for my healing. I had to wrestle out what I knew to be true about my faith—and what a journey it was. Ever since then, receiving communion is always absolutely life changing for me. It's not token or routine but a complete miracle reminder.

From time to time, it's good to sit and contemplate the price that Jesus paid for us all at Calvary. When Jesus hung on that tree, it wasn't only for all the "good" people, or for everyone else. No, He powerfully demonstrated a love like no other when He died for us all, even those who were part of His crucifixion. He died for all.

This was Jesus' illustration to us of what love actually looks like. It is challenging and stunning. His choice to love even those who hurt Him is the way the Bible tells us that the world will know that we follow Jesus: by our love for others.

> The cup of blessing which we bless, is it not the communion of the blood of Christ? The bread which we break, is it not the communion of the body of Christ? For we, though many, are one bread and one body; for we all partake of that one bread. (1 Cor. 10:16–17 NKJV)

The Message version reads like this:

> Because there is one loaf, our many-ness becomes one-ness—Christ doesn't become fragmented in us. Rather, we become unified in Him. We don't reduce Christ to what we are; He raises us to what He is. (v. 17 MSG)

This is the *Lord's* table, and everyone who belongs to Him has a right to partake here, regardless of other labels that may be ascribed. We have equal access. This is an equal opportunity table.

The world will know that we follow
Jesus by our love for others.

Unity cost Jesus everything. As God was raising Him, He was also raising us. Death to life, chaos to calm, lonely to family, judgement to forgiveness.

> It was about the sixth hour, and there was darkness over all the earth until the ninth hour. Then the sun was darkened, and the veil of the temple was torn in two. And when Jesus had cried out with a loud voice, He said, "Father, into Your hands I commit My spirit." (Luke 23:44–46 NKJV)

In life and in death, Jesus was submitted to the Father. As I ponder this thought, every time I come before Him, I also feel compelled to bring the whole of my heart and ask the Lord to reveal the things in me that still need resurrecting. In my fallen state, there are parts of me that want to cling to independence, and there is a very real wrestling with myself and the way I view others. But the cross asks me to look at things differently.

When God gave us the gift of freely expressing our devotion to Christ, it was a gift of incomparable cost.

> When Jesus had cried out again in a loud voice, he gave up his spirit. At that moment the curtain of the temple was torn in two from top to bottom. The earth shook, the rocks split and the tombs broke open. The bodies of many holy people who had died were raised to life. (Matt. 27:50–52)

Everything that had separated us from God was never again to be an issue. Up until that point, there was so much law in the way of personal worship, despite how King David had challenged everything in the way worship was expressed. Jesus still had to make a way so that God's presence was now not in a place for us to go to but was now amongst us, in us, and through us. Access to Him would never again be determined by *our* actions but by *his* goodness.

"Through Jesus, therefore, let us continually offer to God a sacrifice of praise—the fruit of lips that openly profess his name" (Heb. 13:15).

Every time we worship Jesus, we remember the power of the cross and the incredible image of that torn veil. The thing that had separated us from personal intimacy and relationship with God now was torn, and *is* torn, from top to bottom. There is no longer a barrier to keep us from entering the most holy place. In fact, Hebrews 10 says we can boldly enter the throne room of God. Why? Not because of my goodness or lack thereof. But because of the blood of Jesus.

Remember, communion always involves remembering and celebrating all that Jesus has done and won for us personally. It is to be a time when we thank and honour Jesus for all that He has won for us by His shed blood and broken body.

I *love* that when we break the word *communion* down, it carries the idea of a "common union," a table for all.

This common union happens too when we worship in song. When we begin to lift our voices *together* by faith, there is a declared unity that is similar to what happens when we eat, drink, and remember together at the table. It is part of our common inheritance. This is communion, where we celebrate the finished work of Christ.

How do you perceive receiving communion? Is this important to your faith?

At the Cross
You tore the veil,
You made a way,
When You said that it is done

By Darlene Zschech and Reuben Morgan

Day 10

It Is You

A number of years ago, during the hottest summer Australia had experienced in years, there were ferocious bushfires all over the country. Our cities were doing their best to fight off the deadly flames. People and animals were running away from the flames just as fire brigades bravely ran toward them. There were quite a few times over that season when I felt fear trying to creep in, as ash and smoke blocked our view and covered over homes.

Anytime we cannot see the way forward—physically, spiritually, or emotionally—what do we do? It's so easy to panic. I have panicked plenty of times, trying to get my thoughts together to find a way forward. I learned while going through chemo how to pop my hand over my heart, take deep breaths, slow down, and pray.

God is our refuge and strength, an ever present help
in trouble.

Therefore, we will not fear, though the earth give
      way and
the mountains fall into the heart of the sea,
Though its waters roar and foam and the mountains
      quake
with their surging.
There is a river whose streams make glad the city of
      God, the
holy place where the Most High dwells.
God is within her, she will not fall; God will help
      her at daybreak.
Nations are in uproar, kingdoms fall; He lifts His
      voice, the earth melts.
The LORD Almighty is with us; the God of Jacob is
      our fortress.
Come and see what the Lord has done, the
      desolations He has
brought on the earth.
He makes wars cease to the ends of the earth. He
      breaks the
bow and shatters the spear; He burns the shields
      with fire.
He says, "Be still and know that I am God; I will be
      exalted among
the nations, I will be exalted in the earth."

The LORD Almighty is with us; the God of Jacob is
our fortress. (Ps. 46:1–11)

The first two words in this psalm should bring us confidence: *God
is.* God is our refuge, God is our strength, and God is our *ever present*
help. *God is.*

It's in times of crisis when we find out what we really believe about
God—and if we truly believe He is all He says He is. Every time I am
confronted with fear, I also have a choice whether or not to allow the
Lord to take me that little bit deeper in my trust life. When I do welcome Jesus into these seasons, my understanding of God's nature and
presence is made even more tangible in me.

> It's in times of crisis when we find out
> what we really believe about God.

The words of Psalm 46 draw our attention to the nearness of God
in hard times. He's closer than your closest friend or relative, and even
more present than the trouble itself. I'll never forget, just after my dad
died, that overwhelming sense of loss and sadness that felt way too much
to bear. I was at the clothesline crying out to God, when I literally felt the
arm of God come around my shoulder to comfort me. He was literally
very present, pulling me close as I wept, coming at just the right time.

Though the trials of life will come, and though at times you will walk through the fires, you stand by the grace of God. And as the Scripture tells us, for even when heaven and earth pass away, even then, *God is!*

> *This treasure that I hold*
> *More than finest gold*
> *It is You, Jesus*
> *It is You*

Listen to this great quote (from Spurgeon, of course!): "Evil may ferment, wrath may boil, and pride may foam, but the brave heart of Holy confidence trembles not."[4]

The psalmist declares these three precious words: "Come and see." Come and see what God did to overthrow my enemies. Come and see the faithfulness of God in my life. Our confidence in God grows every time we tell our story. It expands every time we share with someone else God's goodness toward us, even in the tiniest things.

There are thousands of scriptures that tell the story of God's miracle provision, salvation, and healings. I mean, every story of God's character leaves me asking the question, "Why at times do I still hesitate to trust in God?"

This is what I have learned: To truly trust, you've got to let go of trying to work everything out yourself. When we say we trust something, we mean that we put confidence or reliance in it. We must learn to let go and trust God. Sounds easy, I know.

Songs of worship help. Intentional prayer helps.

I found this song by the great Reformer Martin Luther. It is from a book written in 1866 entitled *Hymn Writers and Their Hymns* by S. W. Christophers:

> A sure Stronghold our God is He,
> A timely shield and weapon;
> Our help He'll be and set us free
> From every ill can happen.
> And were the world with devils filled,
> All eager to devour us,
> Our souls to fear shall little yield,
> They cannot overpower us.[5]

Luther's comment on Psalm 46 was this:

> We sing this Psalm to the praise of God, because God is with us and powerfully and miraculously preserves and defends His church and His word, against all fanatical spirits, against the gates of hell, against the implacable hatred of the devil, and against all the assaults of the world, the flesh and sin.

Wow! Our great God is our defence and shield, our ever-present help in times of need. Be confident in His ability not only to hear you but to hold you even as you walk through the fire. Take my word for it, and you will come out not even smelling like smoke.

Listen to "The Cross of Christ."

Day 11

The Cross of Christ

It's been a few years now since Mark and I and a group of friends went to Israel for the first time, and yet I still find it hard to articulate the impact it had on me. And even before we arrived home, we were super keen to go back. It somehow felt like a home away from home.

As I walked where Jesus walked and stood where He would have had some of His most pivotal conversations, my heart kept telling me, "Jesus knew what He was here on earth to do." He said He'd come, "to do the will of him who sent me and to finish his work" (John 4:34b).

God sent His perfect Son to pay a price we could not pay. We could not fulfil the law, we could not atone for our own sin, and we could never find a way to secure our own eternity. So, out of a love we did not deserve, grace stepped in and God gave His very best for us. During our time in Israel, it was like we could feel the confidence of the cross wherever we went.

I learned something fascinating about Jesus' cry of "It is finished!" from the cross (John 19:30). For years, I've known that the Greek word behind "It is finished" was *tetelestai*. But what I learned recently is that this word means not only that the work is finished but also that it is *still in effect* today.

It sounds almost too good to be true, but through the power of the cross, we have confident hope that is greater than any devastation, any hardship and injustice, and even greater than death and the fear of death that at times tries to paralyze us.

Jesus said, "I am the resurrection and the life. He who believes in Me, though he may die, he shall live. And whoever lives and believes in Me shall never die" (John 11:25).

There are two particular moments from the cross that continue to challenge me daily, moments that reflect Jesus and His commitment to loving others. The first is when Jesus makes sure His own mother is looked after, as He knows she will need a home and to be loved well.

> Near the cross of Jesus stood his mother, his mother's sister, Mary the wife of Clopas, and Mary Magdalene. When Jesus saw his mother there, and the disciple whom he loved standing nearby, he said to her, "Woman, here is your son," and to the disciple, "Here is your mother." From that time on this disciple took her into his home. (John 19:25–27)

The second is when Jesus speaks to the thief who is hanging on the cross next to Him.

One of the criminals who hung there hurled insults at Him: "Aren't you the Messiah? Save yourself and us!" But the other criminal rebuked him. "Don't you fear God," he said, "since you are under the same sentence? We are punished justly, for we are getting what our deeds deserve. But this man has done nothing wrong."

Then he said, "Jesus, remember me when you come into your kingdom."

Jesus answered him, "Truly I tell you, today you will be with me in paradise." (Luke 23:39–43)

Through these two displays of divine care, Jesus modelled a life lived serving others until our last breath. This is so foundational to what salvation through Jesus looks like.

I was visiting a very ill friend in hospital recently, and while I was asking about where he was up to in his health journey and how specifically we could pray for him, it was soon apparent that he had been witnessing to the man in the bed next to his. It turned out that my friend had organised pastoral visits and food for this stranger. And he did this before he had had anything sorted out with his own health journey.

This is Jesus on display. Caring, praying, sharing Christ with those around us, no matter how inconvenient it may be for us.

Proverbs 11:25 beautifully says, "A generous person will prosper; whoever refreshes others will be refreshed." God's love is a love that is better than life, a love that will not let you go, a love that continues to lift others.

These are the shadows I choose to live under: the shadow of that empty cross and the shadow of an empty tomb.

Come and see the glory of the Lord
Come into His presence all the earth
Singing hallelujah all the glory all the praise
Every nation, tribe and every tongue
Will declare the work of Christ the Son
Singing hallelujah all the glory all the praise

In giving our lives to Jesus, it's all about relationship with a God who does not give us a to-do list. He creates a to-be list. So rather than getting caught up in works and all the doing, the Holy Spirit just continues to shape us from the inside out. It's relationship not religion. Any doing that happens should flow from our knowing who we are in Christ. Jesus came that we may have life. Anytime we find ourselves stooped down or beaten down by life's circumstances, it's great to realise that even from this position, we can lift someone else up. The power of God's Spirit alive in us is truly that magnificent.

Now, who of us would dare to die for the sake of a wicked person? We can all understand if someone was willing to die for a truly noble person. But Christ proved God's passionate love for us by dying in our place while we were still lost and ungodly!

And there is still much more to say of his unfailing love for us! For through the blood of Jesus we have heard the powerful declaration, "You are now righteous in my sight." And because of the sacrifice of Jesus, you will never experience the wrath of God. So if while we were still enemies, God fully reconciled us to himself through the death of his Son, then something greater than friendship is ours. Now that we are at peace with God, and because we share in his resurrection life, how much more we will be rescued from sin's dominion! And even more than that, we overflow with triumphant joy in our new relationship of living in harmony with God—all because of Jesus Christ! (Rom. 5:7–11)

Even when life's circumstances beat us down, we can still lift someone else up.

Can you think of an example in your own life where even in your own pain, you lifted the life of another?

It's only by the power of the Holy Spirit that we can live out this life of loving others well toward Christ. But this is our commissioning. This is our joy and delight.

Lord, I pray You will open our eyes to opportunities around us to lift the lives of others as we walk out our lives before You.

"For everything, absolutely everything, above and below, visible and invisible, rank after rank after rank of angels—*everything* got started in him and finds its purpose in him" (Col. 1:16 MSG).

Day 12

You Will Make a Way

A little while ago I heard someone say, "You will never be someone who is generous in all your ways until you settle the issue of surrender in your heart." This really spoke to me. I feel as if God is trying to move the church into a new day, but I don't believe we can truly enter this newness until we have fully surrendered all of our lives to Him.

Today, much of our lives is built on survival rather than surrender, which is why many find it hard to trust God with their lives. Especially when it means we have to let go of control and believe God's Word with all that is in our hands and hearts.

Knowing that God will make a way through every roadblock in our lives is the game changer. It may not happen in the way or timing that we would like, but whether we encounter roads or rivers, mountains or valleys, chaos or stillness, He's still Lord of it all. The "something new" we are walking into in these important and history-making days requires us to be people of God's Spirit and power. So when we settle for what is natural or doable or what we can control or even manufacture, we tend to forfeit all that God wants to release.

In his first letter, Peter focuses on the importance of believers bearing up under unjust suffering yet continuing to model the grace and love of God.

> The end of all things is near. Therefore, be alert and of sober mind so that you may pray. Above all, love each other deeply, because love covers over a multitude of sins. Offer hospitality to one another without grumbling. Each of you should use whatever gift you have received to serve others, as faithful stewards of God's grace in its various forms. (1 Pet. 4:7)

As believers, we are instructed to use whatever gift we have to serve others—not to squirrel away everything that could be shared with others so that we look after ourselves. This paragraph asks us to pray, to love each other deeply, and to be hospitable to each other without complaining. The Spirit of the Lord enables us to live supernaturally generous lives without fear, for God loves to remove the limits fear puts on us. Fear limits us, the Spirit of God enlarges us.

God loves to remove the limits
fear puts on us. Fear limits us,
the Spirit of God enlarges us.

I don't believe we were created to withhold what we have been given or to simply look after ourselves. However, the reality is that God will let us settle where we want to settle.

This story from 1 Kings is a great example:

> Some time later the brook dried up because there had been no rain in the land. Then the word of the LORD came to him: "Go at once to Zarephath in the region of Sidon and stay there. I have directed a widow there to supply you with food." So he went to Zarephath. When he came to the town gate, a widow was there gathering sticks. He called to her and asked, "Would you bring me a little water in a jar so I may have a drink?" As she was going to get it, he called, "And bring me, please, a piece of bread."
>
> "As surely as the LORD your God lives," she replied, "I don't have any bread—only a handful of flour in a jar and a little olive oil in a jug. I am gathering a few sticks to take home and make a meal for myself and my son, that we may eat it—and die."
>
> Elijah said to her, "Don't be afraid. Go home and do as you have said. But first make a small loaf of bread for me from what you have and bring it to me, and then make something for yourself and your son. For this is what the LORD, the God of Israel, says:

'The jar of flour will not be used up and the jug of oil will not run dry until the day the LORD sends rain on the land.'"

She went away and did as Elijah had told her. So there was food every day for Elijah and for the woman and her family. For the jar of flour was not used up and the jug of oil did not run dry, in keeping with the word of the LORD spoken by Elijah. (17:7–16)

God needs what we have, not what we don't have. When your hands are full with what you think you need, it's hard for God to fill them with what He knows you need.

The widow of Zarephath, through her pain and lack, remained generous to the core as she opened her home and invited Elijah to her last meal. This decision also opened the whole of her life up to the story of miraculous provision.

What about Hannah? Her arms ached for a child, but through her pain, she trusted and yielded to the will of God. She was a worshipper of God, and she had given to Him the child she was believing God for *long* before she ever held that child in her arms. And after many years, Hannah found herself in the midst of a greater miracle than she could have imagined.

Year after year it was the same—Peninnah would taunt Hannah as they went to the Tabernacle. Each time, Hannah would be reduced to tears and would not even eat.... Once after a sacrificial meal at Shiloh, Hannah got up and went to pray. Eli the priest was sitting at his customary place beside the entrance of the Tabernacle. Hannah was in deep anguish, crying bitterly as she prayed to the LORD. And she made this vow: "O LORD of Heaven's Armies, if you will look upon my sorrow and answer my prayer and give me a son, then I will give him back to you. He will be yours for his entire lifetime, and as a sign that he has been dedicated to the LORD, his hair will never be cut." (1 Sam. 1:7, 9–11 NLT)

The journey to surrender can often be painful. But, as we put our trust in Him and surrender to His mysterious and perfect plans again and again, God promises to always make a way.

You will make a way
When I cannot see a way
You're lighting up the path
As Your presence goes before me
You're the God who goes before me

Listen to "Emmanuel."

Day 13

Emmanuel

The virgin will conceive and give birth to a son, and
they will call him Immanuel. (Matt. 1:23)

Immanuel. I cannot count the times have I personally taken incredible strength from this word. Whether you spell it Immanuel (from the Hebrew) or Emmanuel (from the Greek), it means, "God with us."

Have you ever felt lonely or alone and wondered how your heart could handle one more lap around the sun? I have. Many times, in fact. I am a person who needs people to refuel me. Give me a day in the city surrounded by the hustle and bustle of life, and I am *so* happy! Mark is the opposite. During the COVID season, when we didn't have much person-to-person contact, my hubby was finding his soul coming to life! Ha! God certainly has made each one of us so uniquely.

No matter our personality types, our lives were never meant to be lived without constant fellowship with our mighty God. We all need to know that the author and perfecter of our faith is not sitting at a safe distance from us but is right at our side. What an even greater joy to know that when we said yes to Jesus, we said yes to the Father, the Son, and the infilling of the Holy Spirit within us.

I believe that knowing the truth of this word *Immanuel,* down to the fibre of your being, is a very important part of our maturity as a Christ follower. Right from the beginning of time, in Genesis, we read that God walked *with* Adam and Eve. Our disobedience put distance in there, but God's mercy has always welcomed us back.

In Micah, when the prophet was instructing the people how to love God well, he said we were to, "Act justly and to love mercy and to walk humbly with your God" (Mic. 6:8b).

And when the curtain that separated us from the presence of almighty God in Jesus' day was torn in two at the crucifixion, it meant that never again would followers of Christ have to earn their way to an audience with the One who truly matters. Interestingly, the tearing of the curtain was also a prophetic illustration of the fact that the way people had long approached God had reached its final expiry date.

I am sure you have experienced moments when you question God's timing or purposes. I know I have, especially when He seems SO quiet! In those holy silences, and even though I may not *feel* Him close at a particular time, that does not negate the truth of His miraculous presence with me always.

God Himself is with us. And not just with everyone else, God Himself is with *you*. In the fire, in the valley, on the mountains, in the trenches, as we live by faith, even when we walk away or disobey, when life is at its harshest or at its best ... God is with us.

> *There's no one like Jesus*
> *There's no one like Jesus*
> *Strength in times of weakness*
> *Word in flesh among us*
> *You meet me in my sadness*
> *Walk with me through fire*
> *There's no one like Jesus*
> *Calm in every storm*

When all others walk out, He remains the same. He doesn't leave when the going gets tough. He doesn't feel uncomfortable even if we do. He doesn't break eye contact when someone you feel is more significant than you walks into a room. He is not intimidated by our insecurities. He is ever faithful, even in our weaknesses.

Actually, I find that weakness is not a deterrent to our God in any way, shape, or form.

> He said to me, "My grace is sufficient for you, for my power is made perfect in weakness." Therefore, I will boast all the more gladly about my weaknesses, so that Christ's power may rest on me. That is why, for Christ's sake, I delight in weaknesses, in insults, in

hardships, in persecutions, in difficulties. For when I
am weak, then I am strong. (2 Cor. 12:9–10)

Such is the wonder of God's grace that my weaknesses are almost an
attraction to Him. In the Gospels, the word *Immanuel* expresses a personal and a providential presence. He is fully human and yet fully God.
He is a personal, speaking God who waits to be known fully and deeply.
He is providential: Lord of *all,* past, present and future, miraculous and
all glorious. He is fully capable of holding our world in His hands.

God is with us … *Immanuel.* Never let this truth slip from your
heart or mind. And since the same power that raised Christ from the
dead lives in us, then that miraculous presence is *always* with us. The
gospel of John says:

The Word became flesh and made His dwelling among
us. We have seen His glory, the glory of the one and
only Son, who came from the Father, full of grace and
truth…. No one has ever seen God, but the one and only
Son, who is himself God and is in closest relationship
with the Father, has made him known. (1:14, 18)

Jesus has made God *known*. Take a moment to really think on this
statement. We know Him as we dwell in the Word of God. We know
Him as we listen to Him and talk with Him. We know Him as we
spend time in His presence.

I will always treasure a very real encounter I had with Jesus many years ago on my first day of radiation treatment. I felt—so strongly it was almost physical—that every day as I lay on that bed, that Jesus came and held my hand. And every day of that season, He was faithful to hold my hand as I fought for my life. He held me. Literally. My Immanuel.

Jesus has made God *known*. My heart can hardly contain the majesty of this statement.

Before Jesus returned to the Father, He made this promise to *all of us*: "I am with you always, even to the end of the age" (Matt. 28:20b NLT).

Friend, can you remember a time when you sensed the nearness of God?

Where do you find it easy to meet with Him?

Maybe this is an experience you have never had. Can I encourage you to take the time, to sit and *be* with Him, and expectantly *wait* for your own personal encounter with a God who LOVES to be with you.

Let's start right there. Write down what you sense He is saying. THIS is part of the miracle of being known by God.

Listen to "Beautiful Saviour."

Day 14

Beautiful Saviour

There is a song I have loved to sing over many years. I remember my grandparents singing a version of it in their church. It was then called "Fairest Lord Jesus," written in 1662. Later I came to know it as "Beautiful Saviour," which is a morphed version of the original. That is the version I have recorded on *Testament*.

How do you describe the most magnificent person who has ever lived? Trying to describe the beauty of Jesus is like trying to describe the colours seen within the most beautiful and rarest diamond. From every angle you see something different and equally stunning.

The Bible describes Jesus in the most glorious of ways:

- The Bread of Life
- The One who sustains
- The image of the invisible God
- The name that is above every other name
- The Redeemer

- The King of Kings
- The Lord of Lords
- The Son of the living God
- The Chief Cornerstone
- The Author and Finisher of our faith
- The Lamb of God
- The Good Shepherd
- The Bright and Morning Star
- The way and the truth and the life

... just to name a few.

In Isaiah 33:17, when the prophet speaks of Jesus, he says, "Your eyes will see the king in his beauty."

When C. S. Lewis tried to unpack the glory of God's beauty, he said:

> We do not want merely to see beauty, though, God knows, even that is bounty enough. We want something else which can hardly be put into words—to be united with the beauty we see, to pass into it, to receive it into ourselves, to bathe in it, to become part of it.[6]

Beautiful Saviour. When I think about the beauty of Jesus, I think about His countenance. I think about the glory and kindness we imagine when He spoke to the poor or marginalised. I picture the radiance of His smile when He spoke to children and welcomed them to come close to Him. Or the compassion He modelled for us in so many ways throughout the Gospels. It is true that, "Perfect in beauty, God shines forth" (Ps. 50:2).

In Luke 5 we read a story of a man with leprosy coming to Jesus, and the scriptures say He was filled with compassion, He reached out and touched the man and healed him. What a Saviour!

Beautiful Saviour
King of creation
Son of God and Son of Man
Truly I'd love Thee
Truly I'd serve Thee
Light of my soul
My joy and crown

Proverbs 31 tells us that outward beauty is fleeting, which we all know to be true. This world will try to tell you what is beautiful and will also try to sell you beauty at any cost. The Western world spends billions of dollars every year to beautify the outward appearance; and to try to find, develop, and sell a way for this beauty to be made available through external applications.

So what was it that the Bible refers to as the true beauty of Christ?

Isaiah 53 says of the promised Messiah, "He had no form or majesty that we should look at him, no beauty that we should desire him.

He was despised and rejected by men, a man of sorrows and acquainted with grief" (vv. 2b–3a ESV).

The beauty of Jesus was not external. It was the beauty of God in flesh amongst us. When the glory of God rests on any one of us, the beauty of His presence is something to which nothing else can compare. The beauty that Scripture highlights is about the glory and love of God in us and upon us, at work in and through our lives.

We are each a visible display of God's craftsmanship. When His mercy is on display through us every day, this is a kind of beauty that cannot be bottled or bought in a store. You may think you are too tall, too short, or too this or too that. Trust me when I say that the media play on all of our insecurities—for their monetary gain. But God has said that whosoever believes in Him will always be welcome to come close to Him and receive His life-changing love. It's in that proximity to Him that we become not only aware of but also changed by the beauty of God's presence.

> When the glory of God rests on any one of us, the beauty of His presence is something to which nothing else can compare.

I know it is easy to feel disconnected from God at times in the chaotic world we live in. I know it's possible to feel that maybe God is too busy to come near to us or is even concerned with our being filled with His presence. But I love this reminder from Scripture:

> At the center of all this, Christ rules the church.
> The church, you see, is not peripheral to the world;
> the world is peripheral to the church. The church
> is Christ's body, in which he speaks and acts, by
> which he fills everything with his presence. (Eph.
> 1:22–23 MSG)

The church. You and I. The bride. Christ's body. His hands and feet. The beauty we are entrusted with is the glory of His presence. It's our defining feature. It's how a world without the Bible in its hand will see the Bible *alive* in us.

As Paul wrote in Colossians 1:27: "To them God has chosen to make known among the Gentiles the glorious riches of this mystery, which is Christ in you, the hope of glory."

Can you think of a time when someone noticed something different about you?

Perhaps they had no words to describe it, but they noticed how you made them feel. Maybe it was your countenance. Maybe it was because of the way you treated them. Maybe you reached out with compassion when others had just walked on by.

Our beautiful Saviour, Jesus Christ, His resurrection life alive in us, will impact those around us. Take the time to think on the gift of His beautiful presence today and thank Him for the honour of allowing you to share in such a wondrous beauty. It's a beauty that the longer you know Him, the more you reflect.

Listen to "My Confession."

Day 15

My Confession

I've heard it said that your words frame your world. I have seen this statement come true many, many times, both in my own life and in others' lives. One of our dear friends once said to us, "Be careful how you speak about people when they are not in the room, for those you dishonour will eventually leave your life." I have also seen this come to pass.

I also know that people can put words in your mouth. It's as if some people listen to the words you speak with their filters! You cannot help this.

But there is a manner of speech and confession that is honouring to God and His purpose over your life. It's the way of the Spirit. Consider these two verses:

> Finally, brothers and sisters, whatever is true, whatever is noble, whatever is right, whatever is pure,

whatever is lovely, whatever is admirable—if anything is excellent or praiseworthy—think about such things. (Phil. 4:8)

The [intrinsically] good man produces what is good *and* honorable *and* moral out of the good treasure [stored] in his heart; and the [intrinsically] evil *man* produces what is wicked *and* depraved out of the evil [in his heart]; for his mouth speaks from the overflow of his heart. (Luke 6:45 AMP)

So what we dwell on will eventually come out of our mouths. How are you with guarding your words?

I love that Jesus had this type of life-giving reputation in His hometown: "All spoke well of him and were amazed at the gracious words that came from his lips. 'Isn't this Joseph's son?' they asked" (Luke 4:22).

The song "My Confession" is filled with statements about the truth of God's ways and heart toward His people. By putting it to music, we give these ideas a way to stick to your soul so you can recall them when you need them. That's one of the glorious things about worship in song: to combine Scripture and melody in the miracle of song! Oh, how grateful I am.

This is my confession
To this I will hold firm
The Lord is good forever
And His faithfulness endures
Your mercy overflowing
There's nothing I could earn
This is my confession

In Psalm 19, David was reminding himself (and now us) of what the true-north values were that framed his world:

The law of the LORD is perfect, refreshing the soul.
The statutes of the LORD are trustworthy, making
    wise the simple.
The precepts of the LORD are right, giving joy to the
    heart.
The commands of the LORD are radiant, giving light
    to the eyes.
The fear of the LORD is pure, enduring forever.
The decrees of the LORD are firm, and all of them are
    righteous.
They are more precious than gold, than much pure gold;
they are sweeter than honey, than honey from the
    honeycomb.

By them your servant is warned; in keeping them
    there is great reward.
But who can discern their own errors? Forgive my
    hidden faults.
Keep your servant also from willful sins; may they
    not rule over me.
Then I will be blameless, innocent of great
    transgression.
May these words of my mouth and this meditation of
    my heart
Be pleasing in your sight, LORD, my Rock and my
    Redeemer. (Ps. 19:7–14)

David is aware of his own frailty here. He even asks God to forgive him for the things in his blind spots. Wow, we all have blind spots! It's why deep family and friend connections and a great community of faith are so needful when it comes to having a bit of personal accountability—because there are things to confess that we ourselves do not see. This prayer of David's really ramps this thought up. His request to God is that the words of his mouth and the thoughts of his heart would be pleasing to the Lord.

C. S. Lewis said something profound (of course) on this topic: "I have often repented of speech, but hardly ever of silence."[7]

That's a great reminder of the weight of our words and to be careful when using them. However, there is sometimes a different kind of cost related to misplaced silence.

> "I have often repented of speech, but hardly ever of silence." (C. S. Lewis)

We understand that there is an enemy. He works in ways he always has. His purpose is to steal, kill, and destroy. One of the many times he will try to do this is when you need to bring godly language and confession to the table. He will try to cause you to stay *silent*. For example, you can see him starting to try to mess with Jesus around what He knew to be true of His Father.

> Then Jesus was led by the Spirit into the wilderness to be tempted by the devil. After fasting forty days and forty nights, He was hungry. The tempter came to Him and said, "If you are the Son of God, tell these stones to become bread." Jesus answered, "It is written: 'Man shall not live on bread alone, but on every word that comes from the mouth of God.'" Then the

devil took him to the holy city and had him stand on the highest point of the temple. "If you are the Son of God," he said, "throw yourself down. For it is written: 'He will command his angels concerning you, and they will lift you up in their hands, so that you will not strike your foot against a stone.'"

Jesus answered him, "It is also written: 'Do not put the Lord your God to the test.'" Again, the devil took him to a very high mountain and showed him all the kingdoms of the world and their splendor. "All this I will give you," he said, "if you will bow down and worship me." Jesus said to him, "Away from me, Satan! For it is written: 'Worship the Lord your God, and serve Him only.'" Then the devil left him, and angels came and attended him. (Matt. 4:1–11)

Jesus just kept confessing truth over the lies, reminding the enemy where the authority actually rests.

This is *so* intentional. *So* powerful. And so *doable*!

I wonder how often we have lost our dominion due to the wrong timing of our silence. Maybe we stay quiet, thus letting doubt take the lead over our calling. Or maybe we choose nice and tidy expressions of service, rather than lives laid down for the sake of Christ.

Adam lost dominion due to silence. He never spoke up.

Mordecai said to Esther, "If you remain silent at this time ... you and your father's family will perish" (Est. 4:14a).

Let us pray David's prayer ourselves. *May the words of my mouth, and the meditation of my heart, be acceptable in your sight, oh God.*

Listen to "My Jesus, I Love Thee"

Day 16

My Jesus, I Love Thee

This now-classic hymn was originally written in 1864 as a poem by a sixteen-year-old new believer named William Featherstone. I find the intensity of the lyrics and revelation of God's Word astounding, and further proof that this young man truly did encounter the love of God in a way that transformed his life forever.

We don't know much more of Featherstone's short life, as he died at the age of twenty-seven. Apparently, several years after he died, his aunt mailed the poem to Adoniram Judson Gordon (not to be confused with his namesake, Adoniram Judson, a famous missionary). Gordon was a musician and hymn writer. He added a melody to Featherstone's words and had the song published.

It's so wonderful when writers craft songs of adoration that give voice to our heart's cry to God. One thing I cherish about this particular hymn is that Featherstone drew inspiration from these words in 1 John 4:19: "We love because he first loved us."

Because our great God so wildly and wholly loves us, we have the honour of coming before Him with thanksgiving and adoration. This is where worship springs from: our response to His love and mercy.

There is a woman in the Scriptures with whom I've always been fascinated. Her response to the love of Jesus challenges and captivates me every time I read about it. This woman's name turns up quite a few times in the Gospels. She intentionally positioned herself near Jesus during His darkest and hardest hours. She is mentioned fourteen times in the Gospels, and after encountering the love of Jesus, she became completely devoted.

Her name is Mary Magdalene. After the first moment of *seeing* and *experiencing* Jesus, she was never the same. She welcomed Jesus into the centre of her world from that day on.

> After this, Jesus traveled about from one town and village to another, proclaiming the good news of the kingdom of God. The Twelve were with him, and also some women who had been cured of evil spirits and diseases: Mary (called Magdalene) from whom seven demons had come out; Joanna the wife of Chuza, the manager of Herod's household; Susanna; and many others. These women were helping to support them out of their own means. (Luke 8:1–3)

Her name gets confused with other Marys around at that time, but the word *Magdalene* describes her as being from the city of Magdala. We can assume that she had some level of wealth, as she helped to financially support Jesus' ministry. The Bible doesn't say whether or not she was married, but it does tell us she was free to go wherever she wanted to or was prompted to go. In that time and culture, this suggests that she was not married. She is often identified as the "sinful woman" in Luke 7, but there is no conclusive evidence that this is the same woman.

The Bible *does* tell us she had been severely demonically afflicted before meeting Jesus. Seven evil spirits controlled her life and behaviour. This probably would have caused her to be cast to the side of society. We have no real idea of her life or the trauma she may have endured. But we do know that the torment within her was finally silenced by the One who holds *all* authority. When she met Jesus, Mary Magdalene was saved and freed from a very real form of hell on earth.

Her troubles didn't end with her healing, though. She would have had to battle what people around her thought of her, and now as a woman who was free, she had to find her own new normal. But she committed herself to following the One who had delivered her.

No matter what is going on in your life, allowing the life of Christ to dwell in you richly is the only way to walk in eternal freedom. I often think about William Featherstone and what his previous life had been like. What had his childhood been that such a young man could write so eloquently of his death-to-life experience? When we allow our past, our shortcomings, our mistakes, or our failings to dominate our thoughts, we can easily get diverted into responding based on how we feel about ourselves rather than fixing our gaze on Jesus. Ultimately, He takes broken lives and puts them back together. Our weaknesses or scars do become another way to share of God's faithfulness and how He delights in making all things new.

> Allowing the life of Christ to dwell
> in you richly is the only way to
> walk in eternal freedom.

As for us, we have all of these great witnesses who encircle us like clouds. So we must let go of every wound that has pierced us and the sin we so easily fall into. Then we will be able to run life's marathon race with passion and determination, for the path has been already marked out before us.

We look away from the natural realm and we fasten our gaze onto Jesus who birthed faith within us and who leads us forward into faith's perfection. His example is this: Because his heart was focused on the joy of knowing that you would be His, He endured the agony of the cross and conquered its humiliation, and now sits exalted at the right hand of the throne of God! (Heb. 12:1–2 TPT)

This scripture is incredible. God's heart is focused on the joy of knowing we would be His! This is where our understanding of our true worth comes from.

> *I love You Jesus*
> *I'll always love You*
> *Now and forever*
> *I belong to You*

We find Mary *so* dedicated to Jesus that His purpose became *her* purpose. Once she truly encountered Jesus, she was never the same again. Mary became so committed to Jesus that she repeatedly found ways to make sure she could *see* Him.

- Mark 15:40: "Some women were watching from a distance. Among them were Mary Magdalene."
- Mark 16:9: "When Jesus rose early on the first day of the week, he appeared first to Mary Magdalene, out of whom he had driven seven demons."
- John 20:18: "Mary Magdalene went to the disciples with the news: 'I have seen the Lord!' And she told them that he had said these things to her."

I can just imagine Mary with this hunger to not let hope out of her sight. Reading the lyrics of "My Jesus, I Love Thee," I hear the same hunger and devotion in worship.

How do we truly *see* Jesus rather than focusing on all the things we see in ourselves? How do we continue to remember all that Christ has done for us rather than all the things we'd love to forget?

Let me remind you of Psalm 46:

> God is in the midst of his city, secure and never
>   shaken.
>   At daybreak his help will be seen with the
>   appearing of the dawn.
>   When the nations are in uproar with their
>   tottering kingdoms,
>   God simply raises his voice,
>   and the earth begins to disintegrate before him.
>   Here he comes!
>   The Commander!
>   The mighty Lord of Angel Armies is on our side!
>   The God of Jacob fights for us!
>   Pause in his presence
>   Everyone look!
>   Come and see the breathtaking wonders of our
>   God.

For he brings both ruin and revival.
He's the one who makes conflicts end
throughout the earth,
breaking and burning every weapon of war.
Surrender your anxiety.
Be still and realize that I am God.
I am God above all the nations,
and I am exalted throughout the whole earth.
Here he stands!
The Commander!
The mighty Lord of Angel Armies is on our side!
The God of Jacob fights for us! (vv. 5–11)

The answer is always found in knowing the strength of God's Word. This psalm says that His help will be *seen*. It challenges us to surrender so we can see that He is God. It invites us to "Come and see that I am God."

What do you do if you feel like God hasn't kept His side of the bargain?

Can you think of a time when you felt disappointed with an outcome you felt God could have turned around in a different way? What did you do with that? Take the time now to talk to Him about that.

Charles Spurgeon said:

> We shall never find happiness by looking at our prayers, our doings, or our feelings; it is who Jesus is, not what we are, that gives rest to the soul. If we would desire to at once overcome Satan and have peace with God, it must be by "looking unto Jesus."
>
> Keep thine eye simply on Him; let His death, His sufferings, His merits, His glories, His intercession, be fresh upon your mind; when thou wake in the morning look to Him; when thou lie down at night look to Him. Oh! let not thy hopes or fears come between thee and Jesus; follow hard after Him, and He will never fail thee.

He will never fail you, my friend. My prayer for you today is that even if you may feel stuck in your past failings, or even past successes, I pray that you keep your eyes on Jesus. There is no one who loves you more.

Day 17

Worthy Is the Lamb

Then I looked and heard the voice of many angels, numbering thousands upon thousands, and ten thousand times ten thousand. They encircled the throne and the living creatures and the elders. In a loud voice they were saying:

"Worthy is the Lamb, who was slain,
 to receive power and wealth and wisdom and
  strength
 and honor and glory and praise!"

Then I heard every creature in heaven and on earth and under the earth and on the sea, and all that is in them, saying:

"To him who sits on the throne and to the Lamb
    be praise and honor and glory and power,
      for ever and ever!" (Rev. 5:11–13)

My heart seems to expand a little every time we worship Jesus with these words: "Worthy is the Lamb." I get a sense of the thunderous worship the Bible tells we will experience when we join with the voices of ten thousand times ten thousand (and more) angels, declaring praise, honour, glory and power to the Lamb of God.

The simplicity of "Worthy Is the Lamb" came about as I was looking for a song to share in communion as a church family. In a way similar to how I wrote "Shout to the Lord," this song came quickly. All I really wanted to do was to help our church say, "Thank You for the cross, Lord."

When we start digging into the Old Testament, we find that God had established a system that called for the sacrifice of a lamb every morning and evening in Jerusalem to atone for people's sin. Without the shedding of blood, there could be no forgiveness.

"But now in Christ Jesus you who once were far off have been brought near by the blood of Christ" (Eph. 2:13 ESV).

Lambs symbolize innocence, gentleness, and purity. This was the prophetic picture given to us of Jesus, "the Lamb of God, who takes away the sins of the world!" (John 1:29).

Jesus came as the perfect sacrifice provided by God, for the once-and-for-all atonement of sin for humanity.

> He was pierced for our transgressions, he was crushed for our iniquities; the punishment that brought us peace was on Him, and by His wounds we are healed. We all, like sheep, have gone astray, each of us has turned to our own way; and the LORD has laid on Him the iniquity of us all. (Isa. 53:5–6)

Believing that Jesus' sacrificial death on the cross for our sakes is something that is foundational to our salvation, knowing that He made the ultimate sacrifice to bridge the gap between a lost and sinful humanity and a perfect, holy, and loving God.

Worthy is the Lamb
Seated on the throne
We crown You now with many crowns
You reign victorious!
High and lifted up
Jesus, Son of God
The darling of Heaven, crucified
Worthy is the Lamb

The praise that erupts throughout Scripture and culminates in Revelation is so very powerful, and around the throne we see the whole of creation responding by singing, "Worthy is the Lamb." Part of our life of worship is responding in song. This response is from the created to the Creator. When we get a revelation of all Christ has done for us on the cross, that response of adoration encompasses the whole of our lives and includes our songs of worship and devotion.

How long has it been since you took time to sit with Jesus and say thank You for the cross? How long since you last encouraged your soul to bring praise that is authentic from you to Him? God loves it when we take the time to draw near to Him.

As a mum of adult children, there's nothing that blesses me more than one of my kids calling and saying "Mum, want to hang out for a bit?" (for Zoe, it will always be, "Mum, shall we hit Kmart?"). When our children desire time with us, this warms our hearts so deeply that it really doesn't matter what we are doing. It's the care and taking the time to do something together that really fills the love tank.

Because we are made in the image of God, I think He is like this too. How it blesses Him when we want to be with Him, when we stand and sing and declare His name, when we come and pray and spend time with Him, when we lift the life of another, and when we meditate on His Word and find Him in the Scriptures. And with all of it, the heart of God is moved.

How it blesses God when we
want to be with Him.

The Lamb of God removed the barriers so we may come before God anytime and anywhere. But while we may not say it outright, at times it's like we try to put the barriers back up. We can rationalize away the love of God, thinking of all the reasons why we may be disqualified from God's presence and perfection.

Do you ever feel like this?

My encouragement to you on this day is to take some time to simplify your worship with a heartfelt cry of "Worthy is the Lamb." Think on the price that was paid for you. Think on the heart of love that is beating for you right now from the God of heaven and earth. Think on the fact that you are now the righteousness of God in Christ Jesus (see 2 Cor. 5:21).

A. W. Tozer wrote this in *The Pursuit of God*:

> Believing, then, is directing the heart's attention to Jesus. It is lifting the mind to "behold the Lamb of God," and never ceasing that beholding for the rest of our lives. At first this may be difficult, but it becomes

easier as we look steadily at His wondrous Person, quietly and without strain. Distractions may hinder, but once the heart is committed to Him, after each brief excursion away from Him the attention will return again and rest upon Him like a wandering bird coming back to its window.[8]

Listen to "Cry of the Broken"

Day 18

Cry of the Broken

The devastated cry from a young wife as her husband breathed his final breath after a tragic accident is a cry I will never forget. The harrowing cry of a young couple as they lay their newborn to rest after an unexplainable tragedy at birth is also a cry I will never forget. I can still hear the cry of a young, orphaned child in Rwanda as he weeps for his mum and refuses to be held as he safekeeps his heart for her return. These are cries that are so difficult to erase.

The song "Cry of the Broken" was written as a response to this kind of pain and from my own heart's cries. We each endure a lifetime of joys and sorrows that Scripture reminds us that God does not ignore. In fact, the Bible tells us that He bottles every tear (Ps. 56:8 NKJV). The cry of a humanity with no hope was the cry that moved God to send his Son to pay a price for us that we could not pay. Out of His love for us, He came to make a way where there was no way. That's the heart of our God.

You're the mender of the broken
To every outcast
A friend and comforter
We are desperate for Your presence
We are helpless here without You God

Unfortunately, this life is filled with sorrow. Personally, corporately, locally and globally, we will all at some time experience the grief that accompanies loss, tragedy, disappointment, and betrayal. As people of faith who long to see God's goodness outworked in ways our humanness can understand, how do we walk through these seasons of grief and darkness with authenticity whilst holding on to hope? Jesus Himself cried out to the Father as He hung on the cross, "My God, my God, why have you forsaken me?" (Ps. 22:1a).

This psalm and many like it are called psalms of lament. These are psalms that give voice to the gap between our pain and God's promises. At least one third of the Psalms are psalms of lament. These psalms *cry out*, they question, they beat their fists in frustration. Psalms of lament describe our human condition in ways we have all experienced in varying degrees.

As a musician, it blows my mind that God has given us minor chords. These melancholy tones musically and miraculously give voice to these deep emotions that we will all wrestle with on this journey of life. This is where we find the grace, the beauty, and the fortitude of lament.

Perhaps you have grown up in an environment that gives no space or time for grief or lament. Perhaps you have been taught that feeling sadness implies that you are not living in faith. If so, I am going to push back on that thought.

You may find, like I did, lament is a challenge at the start. I remember, after losing my dad to cancer many years ago, that the pastor simply said, "Oh, well, he is with Jesus now. Cheer up!" Truly, there is a part of my heart that does know that and takes comfort in that. But how wrong to put a lock on the large part of the Scriptures and even Jesus' own life that shows Him weeping, questioning God, responding with deep mercy to situations that have grieved His heart. This comment was really more about the pastor's own inability to process grief and finding a trite comment to fill the space that unanswered questions, pain, and grief bring.

Psalm 18 shows us God's powerful arm and support in our distress:

> He reached down from on high and took hold of me;
> He drew me out of deep waters.
> He rescued me from my powerful enemy,
> from my foes, who were too strong for me.
> They confronted me in the day of my disaster,
> but the LORD was my support.
> He brought me out into a spacious place.
> (Ps. 18:16–19)

Lament is unlike other ways we mourn. It hits differently than tears or sorrow. There is a hope attached to lament that leans into God, that leans into the longing for that day when "He will wipe away every tear from their eyes" (Rev. 21:4a).

When I think of the plight of the world and ask the Lord how I should respond and pray, I am comforted by this Psalm: "The righteous cry out, and the LORD hears them; he delivers them from all their troubles" (Ps. 34:17).

The world aches for relief from human suffering, and Jesus has made a way. The only way. Wars and rumours of wars, famine and genocide, natural disasters and world financial collapse, disease and fear across the earth, gangs rising up, political mayhem ... and this is just the beginning. In both the developed and developing world, the groan is loud and the intensity is real.

So as a Christ follower, even though I am not immune to pain or fear, God continues to show me that His people are born and entrusted with this season in history. To that end, we have the privilege to sit in the pain with Jesus, and to sit in the pain with the people around us, to bring the hope of Jesus into every situation as we carry God's presence and glory to bring the reality of "kingdom come on earth" to every place our feet tread.

We have the privilege to sit in the pain
with Jesus, with those around us, to bring
the hope of Jesus into every situation.

But to do this, I have found myself having to pray, to sing, to be *so* grounded in God's Word, and to know the power of His presence like a shield around my heart, and to be most intentional in doing so. His Word truly is like the healing balm of Gilead to the whole of who I am (interestingly, *Gilead* means "a heap of stones of testimony").

Let the Psalms minister deeply to your heart. Let the ache, the groan, drive you to prayer, and welcome the Holy Spirit as He brings comfort and resolve. "He heals the brokenhearted and binds up their wounds" (Ps. 147:3).

How do you respond to the ache you experience at times?

Is lament an easy response for you?

God's got you, my friend. Just pour out your heart to Him.

Listen to "My Hope."

Day 19

My Hope

We are building our lives on the promises of God. Because his Word is unbreakable, our hope is unshakable. We do not stand on the problems of life or the pain in life. We stand on the great and precious promises of God.[9] (Max Lucado)

We live in an age when we are constantly hearing people's spiritual philosophies. It's the "You do you" generation. Apparently, all religious belief systems, as long as they are sincere and heartfelt, are somehow equal. But Jesus teaches otherwise: "I am the way and the truth and the life. No one comes to the Father except through me" (John 14:6).

This hope that we live with is through Christ. The Bible, our anchor of truth, gives us so many descriptions of who Jesus is. It declares that He is not only our hope, but also that He *is* hope. At our church we say, "Hope is a person, and His name is Jesus."

Who is He? The Word describes this hope through hundreds and hundreds of titles:

- Saviour: "For unto you is born this day in the city of David a Saviour, which is Christ the Lord" (Luke 2:11 KJV).
- Alpha and Omega: "I am the Alpha and the Omega, the First and the Last, the Beginning and the End" (Rev. 22:13).
- Good Shepherd: "I am the good shepherd. The good shepherd lays down his life for the sheep" (John 10:11).

But among my favourites is this one:

- My Hope: "Christ Jesus our hope" (1 Tim. 1:1b).

This is our Jesus. Bringing life and life in all its fullness. All that we need in Him is found as we allow and welcome the Word of God to recreate us. Christ in us, the hope of glory! It is through *Jesus* that we find our ability to live in hope with a glowing confidence in what we believe.

My hope is in the Name of the Lord
Where my help comes from
You're my strength my song

My trust in the name of the Lord
I will sing Your praise
You are faithful

In Matthew 8, we find this amazing story of confident hope:

When he had entered Capernaum, a centurion came forward to him, appealing to him, "Lord, my servant is lying paralyzed at home, suffering terribly." And he said to him, "I will come and heal him." But the centurion replied, "Lord, I am not worthy to have you come under my roof, but only say the word, and my servant will be healed. For I too am a man under authority, with soldiers under me. And I say to one, 'Go,' and he goes, and to another, 'Come,' and he comes, and to my servant, 'Do this,' and he does it." When Jesus heard this, he marveled and said to those who followed him, "Truly, I tell you, with no one in Israel have I found such faith. I tell you, many will come from east and west and recline at table with Abraham, Isaac, and Jacob in the kingdom of heaven, while the sons of the kingdom will be thrown into the outer darkness. In that place there will be weeping and gnashing of teeth." And to the centurion Jesus said, "Go; let it be done for you as

you have believed." And the servant was healed at
that very moment. (vv. 5–18 ESV)

The secret of the centurion's great faith was how much hope he
had in Jesus. With that much hope, all that is left is to say, "Just say the
word, Jesus. I believe!" Jesus said he had never seen such great faith!
What an incredible comment to be made about you by the man from
whom hope originated.

Jesus had a miraculous consistency about Him: His ways, His
words, His actions. He had authority over disease, authority over
nature, authority over time and space, authority over demons, authority over creation, authority over sin, and authority over death.

"Jesus came to them and said, 'All authority in heaven and on
earth has been given to me'" (Matt 28:18). His ways commanded hope
wherever He went. He did not ask for it—He just *was* hope.

Do you have hope in Jesus? Do you need hope in Jesus? It starts
with opening your heart to believe and *taking the steps of faith.*

Once we know and believe with great hope who Jesus is as the
Holy Spirit fills us with revelation, we can know and believe with
great hope who we are in Christ. Belief in Jesus gives us our true
identity, knowledge of our true identity brings security, and security
brings freedom. These are the pillars in our soul which are established
through faith in Jesus.

My prayer is, "Lord, grow a confident hope in me." What does that look like? Maybe just like the centurion who says, "Just say the word, and your servant is healed." Jesus is able to meet you right where you are at, and today I pray that your hope rises because Jesus has all authority to literally breathe life back into every situation.

Have you shrunk back from hope? Do you need to dive back into hope? I do know that disappointments or long-term delay can definitely cloud the way forward.

What is it that is limiting your ability to rise in hope? Maybe this is a great topic to discuss in a life group or with a few trusted friends.

At the end of every service at Hope Unlimited Church (HopeUC), we declare together this blessing from Romans 15, "I pray that God, the source of hope, will fill you completely with joy and peace because you trust in Him. Then you will overflow with confident hope through the power of the Holy Spirit" (v. 13 NLT).

Every single time we say this together, you can feel hope rise in the room. That's what hope does. Our God is the author of hope.

But how do we continue to hope in long seasons of delay?

"Now faith is confidence in what we hope for and assurance about what we do not see" (Heb. 11:1).

Belief in Jesus gives us our true identity,
knowledge of our true identity brings
security, and security brings freedom.

Hope gives our faith a job. Hope lifts our expectation to the various Bible verses that outline the truth we believe rather than simply the facts in front of us. This is where we place our hope. Hope is gutsy. Hope is robust. Hope means yes, things may not turn out the way I would prefer, which is why some people pull away and are happy to live with a more measured understanding of what is available right now. Less hope means living with less risk. But there is a way that leans into the nature of God and confidently sings, "My hope is in the name of the Lord."

I for one am willing to lean heavily on the character of Christ and step over my fears into the great grace of hope. I pray you are too. New days. New Hope.

Listen to "You Will Be Praised."

Day 20

You Will Be Praised

I don't think there's a time in the last twenty years of my life when I haven't leaned heavily on Isaiah 61. There's a mood of praise in the chapter that has always captivated me. In a sense, it's a picture of life in Christ, even in the midst of very real hardship.

Even in the Old Testament, there was a call to praise God with music and song (2 Chron. 30:22, for example). It was to be a joyous sacrifice, a thanksgiving decree, and a call to unity. These times of praise were often surrounded by harsh seasons, and the song of thanksgiving was lifted due to obedience and faith rather than pure celebration.

This is a topic that is important for us all. We must learn how to give praise to God in the midst of the toughest of times and *before* we see our desired outcome. Maybe it's in these night seasons that our choice to lean in toward God reveals a mustard-seed faith that is truly pleasing to Him. What I do know is that the character of God is the bedrock for maintaining our trust in Him in every season, bringing our faith regardless of how that feels or even if it looks foolish to some. God's character is still unchanging.

Watch Him at work in this incredible chapter. And the last two lines get me every time.

> The Spirit of God, the Master, is on me
>> because God anointed me.
> He sent me to preach good news to the poor,
>> heal the heartbroken,
> Announce freedom to all captives,
>> pardon all prisoners.
> God sent me to announce the year of his grace—
>> a celebration of God's destruction of our
>>> enemies—
>> and to comfort all who mourn,
> To care for the needs of all who mourn in Zion,
>> give them bouquets of roses instead of ashes,
> Messages of joy instead of news of doom,
>> a praising heart instead of a languid spirit.
> Rename them "Oaks of Righteousness"
>> planted by God to display his glory.
> They'll rebuild the old ruins,
>> raise a new city out of the wreckage.
> They'll start over on the ruined cities,
>> take the rubble left behind and make it new.

You'll hire outsiders to herd your flocks
   and foreigners to work your fields,
But you'll have the title "Priests of God,"
   honored as ministers of our God.
You'll feast on the bounty of nations,
   you'll bask in their glory.
Because you got a double dose of trouble
   and more than your share of contempt,
Your inheritance in the land will be doubled
   and your joy go on forever.
"Because I, God, love fair dealing
   and hate thievery and crime,
I'll pay your wages on time and in full,
   and establish my eternal covenant with you.
Your descendants will become well-known all
     over.
   Your children in foreign countries
Will be recognized at once
   as the people I have blessed."
I will sing for joy in God,
   explode in praise from deep in my soul!
He dressed me up in a suit of salvation,
   he outfitted me in a robe of righteousness,
As a bridegroom who puts on a tuxedo
   and a bride a jeweled tiara.

For as the earth bursts with spring wildflowers,
and as a garden cascades with blossoms,
So the Master, God, brings righteousness into full
bloom
and puts praise on display before the nations.
(Isa. 61 MSG)

If we wish to experience and release God's nature, we must understand that the Spirit of the Lord *is* upon us. Then instead of the spirit of heaviness, He gives His people the garment of praise: His favour, freedom, healing, and restoration.

A garment of praise is something we put on. It's a choice to clothe ourselves in this way. It will always take faith to proclaim and to announce the heartbeat of praise that has been, and forever will be, proclaimed across the earth! Righteousness, justice, and praise will spring up from the earth.

How well do you go with putting on your garment of praise? Does it ever feel fake? What do you do in those times?

You will be praised
You will be praised
Through every storm
You will remain

In death or in life
I'll not be afraid
In joy or in pain
You will be praised

As we have been reminded again and again, it's time to rise up. We are post-COVID. Our role is to be the felt expression of Christ in the midst of a broken and hurting world. The song and stance of our lives are continually announcing God's goodness, God's nearness, and God's saving grace.

The day before I wrote this, I sat with some of my dear friends as they had just received very bad news. Even in their distress, my friends also told me about a man whom they had been sharing Jesus with and how he was very open to the gospel. I watched my friends literally put on their garments of praise as they shared how life-giving it is to share the mystery and wonder of hope in Jesus with another.

My friend, God inhabits the praises of His people! The fullness and wonder of God inhabits our praise. David wrote Psalm 22 as a prophetic psalm, giving us a picture of Jesus declaring His absolute trust in God. And it's here we find the Messiah ... in His suffering and great distress. He remembers the people and the place of praise, saying, "Our God inhabits the praises of His people!"

The writer of Hebrews tells us, "Through Jesus, therefore, let us continually offer to God a sacrifice of praise—the fruit of lips that openly profess his name" (Heb. 13:15). The apostle Peter unpacks it this way, "But you are a chosen people, a royal priesthood, a holy nation, God's special possession, that you may declare the praises of him who called you out of darkness into his wonderful light" (1 Pet. 2:9).

My Testament *is* Christ. It is through Him and by Him that I am able to bring Him praise.

When the prophet Isaiah declared in Isaiah 61 that righteousness, justice and *praise* would spring up across the earth, he was declaring what is happening *today*. While the earth groans, whilst we all encounter suffering on various levels, Jesus still comes to us in our valleys and gives us time to mourn and time to find Him and know Him in ways we simply cannot understand on the mountain tops. But He never leaves us where He finds us. The Holy Spirit with us comforts us and empowers us to once more put on our garment of praise instead of that spirit of heaviness. This life in Jesus is miraculous.

Luke 4 records how, seven hundred years after Isaiah's prophetic declaration, our beloved Jesus reads from this very scroll. He reads from what we now call Isaiah 61, declaring that what had previously been written as prophecy had now become flesh and blood. Like a prologue that began centuries before, Isaiah announced Jesus' purpose ... and declared our future.

My Testament *is* Christ. It is through Him and by Him that I am able to bring Him praise.

Day 21

Fall Afresh on Me
(Spirit of the Living God)

Among the last recorded words of Jesus were these: "You will receive power when the Holy Spirit comes on you" (Acts 1:8).

As He promised, the Holy Spirit was poured out on the church ... and the church was born.

I think a lot about being *God's church* and being filled with *His Spirit*.

> "In the Last Days," God says,
> "I will pour out my Spirit on every kind of people:
> Your sons will prophesy, also your daughters;
> Your young men will see visions, your old men
>   dream dreams.
> When the time comes, I'll pour out my Spirit
> On those who serve me, men and women both,

and they'll prophesy.
I'll set wonders in the sky above and signs on the
　　earth below,
Blood and fire and billowing smoke,
the sun turning black and the moon blood-red,
Before the Day of the Lord arrives, the Day
　　tremendous and marvelous;
And whoever calls out for help to me, God, will be
　　saved." (Acts 2:17–21 MSG)

My question to the Lord has been, "Lord, as *Spirit-filled and Spirit-fuelled people*, how do we truly be Your church? How can we be Your house of hope to the world in this season? Do we really reflect Your heart for humanity and for every 'whoever' we come across?"

The Holy Spirit is described in the Word of God as Comforter, one who convicts, one who speaks, one who is creative and powerful, a wind, a fire, a flood, one who reassures, one who is always leading us to Jesus, one who includes, and one who heals. But today as I talk about the Holy Spirit and us as His bride, I want to remind us of how God has designed His infilling to capture us from the inside out. In this way, we literally display the character of Christ.

Paul, an apostle of Christ Jesus by the will of God,
in keeping with the promise of life that is in Christ
Jesus,

To Timothy, my dear son:

Grace, mercy and peace from God the Father and Christ Jesus our Lord. I thank God, whom I serve, as my ancestors did, with a clear conscience, as night and day I constantly remember you in my prayers. Recalling your tears, I long to see you, so that I may be filled with joy. I am reminded of your sincere faith, which first lived in your grandmother Lois and in your mother Eunice and, I am persuaded, now lives in you also.

For this reason I remind you to fan into flame the gift of God, which is in you through the laying on of my hands. For the Spirit God gave us does not make us timid, but gives us power, love and self-discipline. So do not be ashamed of the testimony about our Lord or of me his prisoner. Rather, join with me in suffering for the gospel, by the power of God. He has saved us and called us to a holy life—not because of anything we have done but because of his own purpose and grace. (2 Tim. 1:1–9)

Paul wants to remind his dear friend Timothy to fan into flame the gift of God. The more the years march on, the more I know that we each must take responsibility for our own flame. This is not about striving; it is about hunger. May we have an authentic hunger for intimacy with God.

We fan into flame the gift of God's Spirit by reading the Word of God, by praying and waiting on God. We fan it into flame as we enter intimate times of worship and prayer with God, as we listen to hear Him speak, as we step out in faith with *God* and watch Him move in our lives, as we yield to His will, and as we speak His love over others.

God has designed His infilling to capture
us from the inside out. In this way, we
literally display the character of Christ.

My friend, if we don't take the time to draw close to God, we get into striving and trying to outwork a holy calling in our own strength. That's not only futile, but it is also what causes our heart to become calloused and our tongue to become harsh.

Like a wind, like a dove
Like a river, like a flood
Holy Spirit, You are welcome here
Come like oil, come like rain
Like a fire set ablaze

Holy Spirit, come and have Your way
Holy Spirit, come and have Your way

David, in all his humanity, tells of his hunger for God throughout the Psalms. Wonderfully, it is here, in the very human David, where we find God taking the most pleasure in David.

> Here is my servant, whom I uphold, my chosen one
>   in whom I delight;
>   I will put my Spirit on him, and he will bring
>   justice to the nations.
>   He will not shout or cry out, or raise his voice in
>   the streets.
>   A bruised reed he will not break,
>   and a smoldering wick he will not snuff out.
>   In faithfulness he will bring forth justice;
>   He will not falter or be discouraged till he
>   establishes justice on earth.
>   In his teaching the islands will put their hope.
>   (Isa. 42:1–4)

I love how this Old Testament passage is a declaration about Jesus and us as New Covenant people. I have put my Spirit on Him. That's the personal, daily infilling by the Spirit, who fuels each of us for our purpose.

But I also love that Isaiah says that the Lord—and we, too, as we are empowered by Him—has the power to not break bruised things and not snuff out wicks that are barely alight. This too is by the power of the Holy Spirit.

Jesus sees the value in any bruised reed. He even makes beautiful music come from a bruised reed, as He puts His strength (or breath) in it!

A smoking flax (used as a wick in an oil lamp) is good for almost nothing, but Jesus knows it is most valuable when it is refreshed with oil.

Now think about the ones whom we have the honour of ministering the love of Jesus to daily: our neighbours, our co-workers, our families. There are many bruised reeds and smoking flaxes too, and we have the privilege of ministering to them just like the Holy Spirit ministers to us. Are there people you can think of today whom you could bring relief to through the gift of God's sweet and powerful Spirit?

People often associate the Holy Spirit with loud and almost showy expressions of power. But God is not a showman. He is a Saviour, a healer, a friend. And as we grow in our relationship with Him, we grow in the knowledge of our purpose *in* God. Purpose is something that unfolds throughout your life, it is not a one-time event. Through Him, we find constant power to breathe life into things that appear like there's no life left in them.

We need the constant filling of the Holy Spirit in order to be refreshed, to operate in the fruits of the Spirit, and to lovingly tend to the bruised reeds around us.

What do you do to intentionally be refreshed in God?

When our hearts are impacted by the kindness of God, every part of our lives is impacted. So is the way we spend our time. This is what the gospel looks like when it is at work in our lives.

But without that fresh infilling, we too can easily become a bruised reed or a smoking flax. This is where we gather hurts and disappointments, becoming embittered by previous hurt. My friend, we desperately need the Spirit of the living God to fall afresh on us daily.

I pray that today is an invitation to constantly encountering God's Spirit within you, and that His power released from your life will bring hope to those around you.

Listen to "You Are Great."

Day 22

You Are Great

Great is the LORD and most worthy of praise;
> his greatness no one can fathom.
> One generation commends your works to another;
> they tell of your mighty acts.
> They speak of the glorious splendor of your
>> majesty—
> and I will meditate on your wonderful works.
> They tell of the power of your awesome works—
> and I will proclaim your great deeds.
> They celebrate your abundant goodness
> and joyfully sing of your righteousness.
> The LORD is gracious and compassionate,
> slow to anger and rich in love. (Ps. 145:3–8)

The greatest experience I have ever had in this earthly body was giving birth to our children. Wow, just wow.

I remember being pregnant with Amy, our eldest, and being so very nervous. Mark and I had everything readied in the tiny nursery we had created with all the love and care in our hearts. I desperately wanted to do it all so well. When the time came to give birth, I remember the midwife saying, "Just let your body do what it was created to do." As I yielded to the waves of painful yet purposeful contractions, this gorgeous little bundle with a full head of hair finally came into the world. I was holding a piece of the greatness of God in my hands, and our lives shifted to meet the needs of this perfect little gift.

Declaring the words "You are great" to God was oh so easy. Life was fairly simple then. We were working hard and treasuring our tiny human, determined to teach her everything we knew about the things of God. The rhythm of life was saturated in sweetness.

But declaring "You are great" to the Lord when all the wheels are falling off, life is no longer so simple, and you have been stretched and tested beyond what you thought possible ...? Well, this is when your faith is built. This is when "You are great" becomes a powerful declaration of faith and hope, despite how things look right now.

The song "You Are Great" came about when our dear friend Martin Smith flew from his home in the UK to the other side of the world to bring love and support to my family while I was walking through treatment for breast cancer. Martin came with a song of *joy* in his heart, and a song of *hope* for all of us to cling to. This selfless act of love brought so much life to our family as the waves were continually crashing over us. I so appreciated Martin's encouragement to write a song together, as I desperately wanted to craft and declare these words especially for my kids, who were trying hard to find language around what to do when fear is trying to take you down and well-meaning people are saying things that are often very unhelpful.

As Jesus followers, we walk by faith. Not by sight, and not by feelings, fads, trends, or opinions. And as we walk and live *in Christ*, our faith grows. It grows through pain and through valleys. Our tenacity of faith grows as we are stretched. It grows as we experience God's precious relief in the midst of tough times. Truthful worship and honest praise help us keep our eyes fixed on Jesus.

You are great
Greater than the world, has ever seen
Higher than the heavens over me
You are great
No one in this world, can have Your fame
So let the earth declare Your holy Name
Jesus!

Sometimes you've got to declare it, sing it, write it, and read it until you believe it ... and that's okay. This is called *faith*. Songs of worship are such a gift. They take our lives by the heart and lead us to declare God's Word, which is alive and transforming.

> Truthful worship and honest praise
> help us keep our eyes fixed on Jesus.

In our lives thus far, Mark and I have made decision after decision about the call of God on our lives, doing our best to follow His leading. And for the sake of our children and their understanding of God's faithfulness, we have prayed continually that by God's grace, we would have the ability to live out God's call and keep the main thing the main thing.

When I look at King David leading his people in songs of praise, I cannot help but see his passion for the next generation. He shared the stories of God's greatness in his life to them. And God's people continue to relay not just David's stories, but their own, because God's greatness continues throughout all generations. This psalm is a constant dance of generational declarations from one to another, as each joyfully sings and confidently tells the God stories.

If we want this for our own families and churches, then we must intentionally practice the art of telling God's stories to the next generation. That's why songs of praise are so important to sing to our God in the congregational setting, as together every generation unites in song to declare the wonders of God.

"Praise the LORD! Praise God in His sanctuary; Praise Him in His mighty firmament! Praise Him for His mighty acts; Praise Him according to His excellent greatness!" (Ps. 150:1–2 NKJV). (Another way to translate *firmament* is "the expanse of His heavens.")

Do you find this kind of praise easy? Are there opportunities in your life to tell others the stories of when God came and rescued you once more? Look for these opportunities.

If you are someone who journals, then this is a beautiful way to keep a record of these stories. I am a "sometimes" journal keeper. I am probably better at writing my thoughts in a song! But whatever way works for you, why don't you look at how you can begin to share your God stories with others, and then listen to others as they do the same.

Day 23

Mercy Endures

Your love endures forever
Reaches to the heavens
Though my flesh may fail me,
You're the strength of my heart,
You will always be
I know Your lovingkindness
The power of forgiveness
All that I hold dear is Yours
My Jesus, it's You I long for.

There is no better-known psalm than Psalm 23. David, the former shepherd boy, now speaks of God as *his* shepherd. As one who cares, leads, and restores. This beautiful piece of godly poetry is one of great comfort and strength, full of kindness and security. It is a powerful song of safety. And it's where the song "Mercy Endures" originated.

The first verse of the song arises directly from David's words: "Even though I walk through the darkest valley, I will fear no evil, for you are with me; your rod and your staff, they comfort me" (Ps. 23:4).

The last verse in this stunning psalm says, "Surely your goodness and love will follow me all the days of my life, and I will dwell in the house of the LORD forever" (Ps. 23:6).

We speak of mercy often. And rightly so, because mercy flows from the enduring love of God, which literally sustains us through every season of life.

I found this in a commentary:

> Mercy is the covenant-word rendered "steadfast love." Together with goodness, it suggests the steady kindness and support that one can count on between family or close friendships. With God, these qualities are not only solid and dependable, but vigorous—for to follow does not mean to merely bring up the rear, but to PURSUE.[10]

To pursue the heart of God! This is really what our growing up and into Christ is all about. This is discipleship. You can hear the pursuit in David's heart as he pens his longing for and personal experience of God's lovingkindness. The pursuit of Christ is the highest pursuit of our entire lives. Truly, where would we be without the great mercy of our God? He is *faithful* to the end.

"The steadfast love of the LORD never ceases; His mercies never come to an end; they are new every morning; great is your faithfulness" (Lam. 3:22–23).

Love and mercy, love and mercy ... they are like best friends who cannot let go of each other.

They are there for you whether you feel worthy of God's love and mercy or not, and whether or not you even *want* to receive His love and mercy. It doesn't matter how hard you try to tell Him all the reasons why you don't deserve it, God tells us continually throughout His Word that it's *because* of His love for us that this gift is always ours.

It would be like one of my children when they were little, after misbehaving in some way, thinking even for a second that our love for them had changed or grown weaker. *No way.* That would mean my love for them was based on their performance! No.

> When the kindness of God our Savior and His love for mankind appeared, He saved us, not on the basis of deeds which we have done in righteousness, but according to His mercy, by the washing of regeneration and renewing by the Holy Spirit, whom He poured out upon us richly through Jesus Christ our Savior. (Titus 3:4–6)

This love we have received has been freely given to us. It is based on Jesus' sacrifice for us, not the other way around. And there is nothing that will separate us from this love.

I am convinced that neither death nor life, neither angels nor demons, neither the present nor the future, nor any powers, neither height nor depth, nor anything else in all creation, will be able to separate us from the love of God that is in Christ Jesus our Lord. (Rom. 8:38–39)

Is there anything in you that makes you question God's enduring love?

Do you have any reasons not to trust God with your life? Can you call Him your shepherd like David did?

I think these are great questions to ask. On the day I wrote this chapter, I spoke with someone whose family has been battered by serious illness. I asked him how he pictured God in this scenario. He replied, "Without the Lord, without knowing a God who hears me when I pray, I simply do not know how we would have survived the onslaught of evil that tried to take us down."

This love is based on Jesus'
sacrifice for us, not the other
way around. And nothing
will separate us from it.

Not everybody feels this way. People can be quick to blame God for anything bad that happens, not ever understanding that the heart of God breaks with us in our pain and is always at work to bring resolution in one way or another. It's often true, though, that God's timing and our timing are very different. Again, it's why learning to *trust* is so very important to the growth of a Christian.

His love endures forever, friend. When you feel His love and even when you don't, His love *still* endures forever. God made a way for each one of us to become right with Him—not through our works, but according to His great and continual outpouring of love and mercy. It's always good to "calmly think on these things."

I truly pray that as we are recipients of God's incredible mercy we too would be givers of mercy.

Paul addressed this in 1 Timothy:

> Christ Jesus came into the world to save sinners—of whom I am the worst. But for that very reason I was shown mercy so that in me, the worst of sinners, Christ Jesus might display his immense patience as an example for those who would believe in him and receive eternal life. (1:15–16)

My friend, because Jesus endured the cross, He has given us the power to endure whatever we must face in life. Even if your world grows dark and you find yourself feeling abandoned by all you know and love, our God of mercy is there with comfort and healing. You are never alone, never forsaken, and always loved. That is the promise of the cross. Don't ever lose heart. *He has overcome the world.*

Listen to "There Is a Redeemer."

Day 24

There Is a Redeemer

Some days are etched in your memory. This is sometimes for tragic reasons, sometimes for joyful reasons.

I can still remember where I was standing when I heard the news of the tragic plane crash that killed Christian musician Keith Green, two of his children, and some of his friends. His book *No Compromise* had really helped answer some big questions I'd been wrestling with about integrity, ministry, and music.[11] The songs he and his wife, Melody, were writing had an "otherness" to them I couldn't explain. I joined with millions of people around the world as we mourned the death of this feisty trailblazer who truly loved Jesus.

Melody had written a song called "There Is a Redeemer," and Keith had recorded it in the early 1980s. It was one of those songs that ministered to my heart immediately and would not let me go. Over the many years since then, I have seen people respond to the heart of God so powerfully as together we've sung this song in worship. And now for this *Testament* album project, I decided to record it.

I got brave and added a little refrain in my version. I just wanted to add a decree that says ultimately, Love wins. The refrain goes like this:

Love has won
Now I rest in Your promise
As I wait
You are singing over me
Love has come
So we sing with the angels
Hallelujah
To the King of kings.

May He grant you out of the riches of His glory, to be strengthened *and* spiritually energized with power through His Spirit in your inner self, [indwelling your innermost being and personality], so that Christ may dwell in your hearts through your faith. And may you, having been [deeply] rooted and [securely] grounded in love, be fully capable of comprehending with all the saints (God's people) the width and length and height and depth of His love [fully experiencing that amazing, endless love]; and [that you may come] to know [practically, through personal experience] the love of Christ which far surpasses [mere] knowledge [without experience], that you may be filled up [throughout your being] to all the fullness of God [so that you may have the richest experience of God's presence in your lives, completely filled and flooded with God Himself].

Now to Him who is able to [carry out His purpose and] do super abundantly more than all that we dare ask or think [infinitely beyond our greatest prayers, hopes, or dreams], according to His power that is at work within us, to Him be the glory in the church and in Christ Jesus throughout all generations forever and ever. Amen. (Eph. 3:16–21 AMP)

These verses are never far from me. They are foundational to how the love of God impacts everything about our lives. I was especially struck by this version's translation in verse 19 that says we are "flooded with God Himself."

Have you ever been in a real flood?

I remember as a kid when we were in-between houses, all our possessions were in a storage facility, and our family of six was living in a caravan for a season. The infamous 1974 floods in Queensland wreaked havoc upon many people's lives. We were blessed that our caravan was not swept away, but the storage facility had gone underwater. I will never forget when we finally got access to our possessions. I remember my mum and dad going through the wreckage and crying, as everything we owned was ruined. Water gets into every nook and cranny. Nothing escapes being impacted by a flood.

Being *flooded* by God Himself is a pretty intense description. To be flooded with God's presence is to have the richest possible experience of God's presence in our lives.

Jesus walked this out every day in many radical ways.

> When Jesus came down from the mountainside, large crowds followed him. A man with leprosy came and knelt before him and said, "Lord, if you are willing, you can make me clean."
>
> Jesus reached out His hand and touched the man. "I am willing," He said. "Be clean!" Immediately he was cleansed of his leprosy. Then Jesus said to him, "See that you don't tell anyone. But go, show yourself to the priest and offer the gift Moses commanded, as a testimony to them." (Matt. 8:1–4)

Jesus touched the man with leprosy.

In the regions where the Bible was written, those with leprosy were considered the lowest in society. They faced rejection, and most became beggars who lived on the side of the road.

Jesus didn't just see people—He held people. He loved people. He demonstrated *love*.

In our lives, Jesus is not just to be defined but also demonstrated. Being flooded with Christ Himself, we can bring this same life to those around us.

> Christ's love compels us, because we are convinced
> that one died for all, and therefore all died. And He
> died for all, that those who live should no longer live
> for themselves but for Him who died for them and
> was raised again. (2 Cor. 5:14–15)

The love of God is the scaffold from which we live our lives. It is a continual work of the Spirit required in each of us. Oh, in my own strength I run out of love, which is why our daily infilling of God's powerful Word in our lives and the awakening of His Spirit in us is critical.

Jesus didn't just see people—He
held people. He loved people.
He demonstrated *love*.

We often see the word *Redeemer* used to describe Christ. It describes the salvation He accomplished for us. Jesus "bought us back" from captivity, giving us total freedom. Truly, the outworking of God's great love in our lives is far greater than we can imagine.

Psalm 86 says, "He is merciful and gracious, slow to anger, abounding in steadfast love and faithfulness."

John 15:9–17 says, "As the Father has loved me, so have I loved you."

Romans 5:8 says, "God shows His love for us that while we were still sinners, He died for us."

The Beatitudes remind us of all that we receive through the finished work of Christ:

> Blessed are the poor in spirit, for theirs is the kingdom of heaven.
>
> Blessed are those who mourn, for they will be comforted.
>
> Blessed are the meek, for they will inherit the earth.
>
> Blessed are those who hunger and thirst for righteousness, for they will be filled.
>
> Blessed are the merciful, for they will be shown mercy.
>
> Blessed are the pure in heart, for they will see God.
>
> Blessed are the peacemakers, for they will be called children of God.

Blessed are those who are persecuted because of righteousness, for theirs is the kingdom of heaven.

Blessed are you when people insult you, persecute you and falsely say all kinds of evil against you because of me. Rejoice and be glad, because great is your reward in heaven, for in the same way they persecuted the prophets who were before you. (Matt. 5:3–12)

As those who know God's redemption and love, we are asked to make choices to align our values with the Redeemer.

Choosing to be a peacemaker when you feel you have every right to have yourself be heard. The Word says that those who pursue peace will see God.

Choosing to love those who do you wrong. Choosing to embrace the dying, the confused, the outcasts ... this all sounds good. But I believe God will trust us with them only when we are ready to love them like He does. I believe that God, the perfect Father, holds a few things back from His church until we learn how to love certain people well. He just cannot see them hurt any more than they already are. "As long as there is day and night, He will cause mercy, kindness and steadfast love on and for His people" (Jer. 33:19).

My prayer this last couple of years has been, "Please, God, let Your love grow inside of me so that there is *nothing* left of all the things that hold me back from truly loving others with Your love."

Humanity is complicated. *We* are complicated. There are those who are easy to love, but there is only so far you can love someone with your own ability. To love those who have mistreated you, to love those who don't understand you, to love those who persecute you, to love those who live in direct contrast to how a Christ follower lives ... this is the love that really matters. And it will matter more and more as the days get darker across the earth. This kind of love holds fear at bay and breaks through every wall with compassion and God's unshakeable character.

If the church across the earth is not known as a people who truly love, then we will not be representing the heart of God. Our purposed lives really do matter as the love and power of God are continually at work in the very core of who we are.

Maybe take some time to study this word *redeemed* and remember all that God has redeemed you from. Then, ask the Holy Spirit to show you how you can share your own experience with others.

Charles Spurgeon said, "Nothing binds me to my Lord like a strong belief in His changeless love."[12]

Day 25

Forever My King

Light of my heart, Lamp to my feet
Hope of the world, Heaven in me
River of life, deep calls to deep
I'll worship you now and forever my King

When we raised our three daughters, and now as we enjoy our four granddaughters and two grandsons, the world of princes, princesses, and palaces was and is certainly not lost on me. My own children were captivated by these royal titles early in life, probably pushed along by the power of Disney and the lure of marketing. We had tiaras and sparkling gowns, slip-on fancy shoes, and the occasional wand to make sure we could knight anyone we wanted at a moment's notice.

There is something deep within us that has a leaning toward kingdoms. A leaning toward kings and queens. We find throughout history a propensity toward humanity following a regal kingdom.

There are certain expectations and conventions one associates with kings, queens, and all that kingdoms entail.

So when Jesus enters the scene as a baby in a manger, it's no surprise that the people struggle to recognize Him as the promised King.

When He is grown and begins His ministry, the confusion continues. Instead of coming to rule with an iron fist and enjoying all the pomp and ceremony the King of Kings deserves, Jesus comes to us via the most humble circumstances. His rule and reign flow not from might but from a position of love. Rather than a crown, a palace, and an earthly throne, Jesus comes to live amongst us. And rather than avoiding death through supernatural means, as we might expect a heavenly King to do, He dies. He's executed on a wooden cross, His life *given* as the ultimate service to His people. And then, upon His resurrection, we begin to see His power as heavenly King. But is it any wonder that all of this was hard for people to comprehend?

So, what is this kingdom?

> Do you see what we've got? An unshakable kingdom! And do you see how thankful we must be? Not only thankful, but brimming with worship, deeply reverent before God. For God is not an indifferent bystander.
>
> He's actively cleaning house, torching all that needs to burn, and He won't quit until it's all cleansed. God himself is Fire! (Heb. 12:28–29 MSG)

The Word of God tells us that this kingdom is unshakeable. The kingdom where Jesus reigns and love trumps everything.

When I was researching kingdoms across history, I was amazed to learn about all the empires and the kingdoms that have existed throughout the world. Thousands of them, in fact. Some were incredibly strong, rich with land, wealth, military, etc. These were kingdoms you'd have thought were safe. Kingdoms you'd have thought would still be thriving today. But kingdoms come and kingdoms go. Except for this *one* kingdom.

> What is the kingdom of God like, and to what shall I compare it? It is like a mustard seed, which a man took and threw into his own garden; and it grew and became a tree, and the birds of the air nested in its branches. (Luke 13:18–19)

Whenever we say *yes* to the lordship of Christ in our lives, we say *yes* to Jesus as King of our lives, we say *yes* to God's rule, and we say *yes* to the kingdom of God. Just like a mustard seed, the reign of this heavenly kingdom is growing in us, causing us to become more like Christ, which is always the goal.

Just think about it: an unshakeable, triumphant kingdom at work, growing within us. Safe, secure, life giving, immovable, alive, glorious, unshakeable, eternal, and growing.

When we say *yes* to the lordship of
Christ in our lives, we say *yes* to Jesus
as King of our lives, *yes* to God's rule,
and *yes* to the kingdom of God.

This is why when you say *yes* to the love of God in your life, your life begins to move to a different rhythm—a kingdom rhythm. Suddenly, you find yourself not able to go to certain parties or watching certain shows, and you find your heart being moved with compassion in ways that maybe it never has before.

C. S. Lewis said:

> That is why the real problem of the Christian life comes where people do not usually look for it. This Kingdom comes the very moment you wake up each morning. All your wishes and hopes for the day rush at you like wild animals. And the first job each morning consists simply in shoving them all back; in listening to that other voice, taking that other point of view, letting that other larger, stronger, quieter life come flowing in. And so on, all day. Standing back from all your natural fussings and frettings; coming in out of the wind.[13]

I love the idea of Christianity as "that other larger, stronger, quieter life." This is the unshakeable terrain of God's glory. While everything else around the globe right now is being shaken (everything from economic security, to gender security, national security, personal security), the kingdom of God at work within us is the most secure place there is.

> In this manner, therefore, pray:
> Our Father in heaven,
> Hallowed be Your name.
> Your kingdom come.
> Your will be done
> On earth as it is in heaven.
> Give us this day our daily bread.
> And forgive us our debts,
> As we forgive our debtors.
> And do not lead us into temptation,
> But deliver us from the evil one.
> For Yours is the kingdom and the power and the
> glory forever. Amen. (Matt. 6:9–14 NKJV)

God's kingdom come on earth as it is in heaven. Maybe it's time we became more intentional about aligning ourselves a little less with the ceremony and values of earthly kingdoms to align ourselves with God's kingdom. Maybe it's time to ask the Holy Spirit to reveal how we can employ the authority God has given each of us to walk humbly as His children, bringing the values of the kingdom of heaven to earth.

How does this sit with you?

Sometimes it's hard to recognize yourself as being someone who is so valued that the kingdom of God would be entrusted to you. Take time today to think about a time when you were aware of God's kingdom being at work in you. You may be surprised at the things you remember.

"The LORD has established his throne in heaven, and His kingdom rules over all" (Ps. 103:19).

Listen to "Glorify Your Name."

Day 26

Glorify Your Name

I have been writing songs since I was a teenager. I am not even really sure how it came about, except that my family loved music. We are all musicians in some sense, and songwriting became a bit of a hobby. I have shared my story of becoming a Christian, and how afterward my heart really struggled with writing or even singing any songs that were not about the worship of God. To be honest, I knew nothing about what worship even was, except to say that my life was coming into alignment with a different set of values. For me, that included everything I knew about music (actually what I knew about everything).

After a few years of being discipled in the Word of God at my local church, I started really asking God about my design, my purpose on earth. I had some fun times writing and singing songs with a Christian ethos, but it still didn't feel like my "fit."

For some reason, I really thought there was just *one* way to serve the purposes of God. That put a lot of pressure on me. If I didn't do something to do with music, did it mean I was disqualified? How would I live to glorify the name of Jesus if I didn't know what to do or how to do it?

If you ever find yourself confused about what your purpose or mission is, the Bible keeps things clear. Which is good, because we tend to make things complicated (at least I do!).

> You are a chosen race, a royal priesthood, a holy nation, a people for His own possession, that you may proclaim the excellencies of Him who called you out of darkness into His marvelous light. (1 Pet. 2:9 ESV)

This passage is addressed to Christians and simply says God's purpose for us is that we may proclaim His excellencies.

We see here our one gloriously common calling, our one mission, to declare His excellencies. In other words, we are to declare His glory, to be a witness, to tell our story, and to show people Jesus through the whole of our lives, whatever it looks like.

This is the mission we are all made for. Look at it in *The Message* translation.

> You are the ones chosen by God, chosen for the high calling of priestly work, chosen to be a holy people, God's instruments to do His work and speak out for Him, to tell others of the night-and-day difference

He made for you—from nothing to something, from rejected to accepted. (1 Pet. 2:9 MSG)

In John's gospel, Jesus says this to God about His followers: "Just as you sent me into the world, I am sending them into the world" (17:18 NLT).

Jesus, Jesus
On the cross you took my shame
Forever from my heart I'll say
I live to worship You, Lord
My King of glory
Brought me to life
Gave me wings to fly

I believe we have all been born with a personal mission customized for each one of us. There will be aspects of your life lived unto God that only you can fulfil. I also believe we have also been given a gloriously common mission (a *commission*) that we share with the entire body of Christ: sharing the gospel and making disciples. Using the whole of our lives as a spiritual act of worship.

Through Jesus, therefore, let us continually offer to God a sacrifice of praise—the fruit of lips that openly profess his name. And do not forget to do good and to share with others, for with such sacrifices God is pleased. (Heb. 13:15–16)

In the midst of all the praise, the writer of Hebrews is asking us not to forget that there is more to our life than songs and celebration of our faith. Although these are uber important, we cannot have the first half of the script without the second. As a consumer generation, we've got to remember that God is not looking for simply more songs. He is looking for people to be activated in His presence and yielded to the power and glory of almighty God. He's looking for a people who will say *yes* to being His presence-carriers in this world.

The Bible asks us to attend to our worshipful lives, because worship continues to affect and correct our hearts. But the overflow of a worshipful life is a life lived for the glory of God. This is our life of mission.

Tim Tennent, president of Asbury Theological Seminary says, "This is why missions cannot be relegated to merely a task of the church. Missions is the very means by which the church becomes the body of Christ, realizing and manifesting the fullness of Christ."

When I think about the great CO-mission for God's church across the earth, I believe we must think about how those who are not inside our buildings may perceive or experience the church. Jesus said, "A new command I give you: love one another. As I have loved you, so you must love one another. By this everyone will know that you are my disciples, if you love one another" (John 13:34–35).

I am sure we can all do this in an even more intentional way. For starters, be careful what you publicly criticize or become a "keyboard warrior" about. When it comes to our brothers and sisters in Christ, God asks us to pray, to forgive, and to go to them earnestly and privately, with help from others if you need it.

> God is looking for people who will
> say *yes* to being His presence-
> carriers in this world.

It's so life-giving to hear Jesus say that He will be with us as we walk out His mission on the earth through our lifetime. It's not about striving but telling our story and living out what we have experienced of the love of God. It's about mirroring Jesus' actions as we go through this world.

The mission is to serve all with the love of God. We stand against injustice, we speak up for those with no voice, and all of it is done in a posture of service.

Jesus' presence on earth is good news to all people. That's the gospel: the good news.

My challenge today to you and me is to be part of the mission of God. Don't overthink it like I did. No striving required. Love God, love others, serve people, walk in the fruit of the Spirit. Perhaps you could foster a child, sponsor a child overseas, cook a meal for a single parent, start praying intentionally for people by name, or get a bunch of friends together to see what your community leaders are doing—and get involved. Maybe you can be more intentional about being present for your family, your neighbours, your friends, the ones you easily love. Perhaps you can make an effort to love the ones you don't understand. This is a mission *for all, by all*.

How can you be more intentional in your personal life of worship and mission today?

Day 27

Saviour

For almost two thousand years, people have been trying to create songs of worship, paint paintings, choreograph dances, and design and construct buildings to the glory of our resurrected Saviour. No matter how wondrous the result, the truth is that we fall short of the fullness of expression. A song that I wrote many years ago called "Saviour" was the result of trying to do just that.

I was studying Matthew 27 and imagining myself amongst the women who had gathered near the cross. It says they were ministering to the needs of Jesus.

When the centurion and those with him who were guarding Jesus saw the earthquake and all that had happened, they were terrified, and exclaimed, "Surely he was the Son of God!" Many women were there, watching from a distance. They had followed Jesus from Galilee to care for his needs. Among them were Mary Magdalene, Mary the mother of James and Joseph, and the mother of Zebedee's sons. (Matt. 27:54–56)

Today, years later, as I look at the day-to-day rhythms of my life, I seem to find myself asking, "Am *I* ministering to the needs of Jesus?" What can I bring Him that He doesn't already have? But He does seem to love my time spent with Him, my affections toward Him, and my trust in Him. He does not demand these things, but He longs for me to willingly bring them.

Meditating on the cost paid at Calvary teaches my heart to long for more of Him ... and less of me.

Our Saviour, our King of all kings, allowed Himself to be given for us.

They stripped him and put a scarlet robe on him, and then twisted together a crown of thorns and set it on his head. They put a staff in his right hand. Then they knelt in front of him and mocked him. "Hail, king of the Jews!" they said. They spat on him and took the staff and struck him on the head again and again. After they had mocked him, they took off the robe and put his own clothes on him. Then they led him away to crucify him. (Matt. 27:28–31)

Even hanging on the cross, positioned between two thieves who were also being crucified, Jesus continued ministering. He offered forgiveness and eternal life as He fought for every breath. As He fulfilled all the prophecies, as He sweat drops of blood, and even as He felt forsaken by His own heavenly Father, He continued to give up His life so that another could find life in Him eternally.

That's why the lyrics of this song bounce between almost disbelief in all that Christ has won for us.

> *A Saviour on a hill dying for my shame*
> *Could this be true?*
> *Defies the world I see*
> *Yet this is all my heart was longing for*
> *To know You my Lord*
> *To know You Lord*

I love this from Psalm 145: "Great is the LORD and most worthy of praise; His greatness no one can fathom" (v. 3).

Yes, He deserves all the glory and all the praise. That beautiful word *hallelujah* comes rushing in to praise our God joyously. It is the eternal word of response when God's people boast in Him and declare His praise with all they have. Truly, we will need all of eternity to fully unpack the depth of gratitude we each have for the finished work of the cross.

It is good to take the time, to slow down, to breathe deeply and remember this gruelling and complete price paid so each one of us can stand whole, righteous, and free in the presence of our God.

There will be times when this life feels just all too hard, when it feels all-consuming, almost as if the pressure could literally break you. It's when we've come to the end of ourselves that we find the depth of beauty of God's grace.

One of the great gifts God has given us is the powerful sacrament of communion. To take the bread and the wine and give thanks, remembering all He has done for us. To remind our hearts, our emotions, and our souls that "Greater is he that is in you, than he that is in the world" (1 John 4:4 KJV). This is why communion, common union, around the body and blood of our Saviour is so very important.

It's when we've come to the end of
ourselves that we find the depth
of beauty of God's grace.

Is communion something that is important to you? I remember as a child thinking to myself that if the pastor really knew what kind of person I was, he wouldn't allow me to receive it freely as he did. But now I understand communion as a gift to me. I see now that if I was receiving it because I was somehow earning it, then the grace of God would not be needed. And so I partake, aware of my lack, but more aware of God's grace, and thankful to the core of my being.

The cross of Christ, that great intersection between heaven and earth, is a moment in time that shifted our lives forever. Jesus' broken body is our healing. By His stripes I am healed. I don't receive communion because of a tradition but because I believe in the Scriptures that tell me, "'He himself bore our sins' in his body on the cross, so that we might die to sins and live for righteousness; 'by his wounds you have been healed'" (1 Pet. 2:24).

May today be the start of a new chapter in your journey of following Jesus. Commit to partake in communion with a new passion and understanding. And may the joy and wonder of *Hallelujah* give you a way to release constant thanksgiving in your heart and in your home. All for the glory of God.

"God is always coming to you in the Sacrament of the Present Moment. Meet and receive Him there with gratitude in that sacrament" (Evelyn Underhill).

Listen to "Mercy on Display."

Day 28

Mercy on Display

When I think of the word *mercy*, it's hard to walk past the story of the good Samaritan:

> On one occasion an expert in the law stood up to test Jesus. "Teacher," he asked, "what must I do to inherit eternal life?" "What is written in the Law?" he replied. "How do you read it?" He answered, "'Love the Lord your God with all your heart and with all your soul and with all your strength and with all your mind' and 'Love your neighbor as yourself.'"
>
> "You have answered correctly," Jesus replied. "Do this and you will live." But he wanted to justify himself, so he asked Jesus, "And who is my neighbor?" In reply Jesus said: "A man was going down from Jerusalem to Jericho, when he was attacked by robbers. They stripped him of his clothes, beat him and went away,

leaving him half dead. A priest happened to be going down the same road, and when he saw the man, he passed by on the other side. So too, a Levite, when he came to the place and saw him, passed by on the other side. But a Samaritan, as he traveled, came where the man was; and when he saw him, he took pity on him. He went to him and bandaged his wounds, pouring on oil and wine. Then he put the man on his own donkey, brought him to an inn and took care of him. The next day he took out two denarii and gave them to the inn-keeper. 'Look after him,' he said, 'and when I return, I will reimburse you for any extra expense you may have.'

"Which of these three do you think was a neighbor to the man who fell into the hands of robbers?" The expert in the law replied, "The one who had mercy on him."

Jesus told him, "Go and do likewise." (Luke 10:25–37)

I have read this story a thousand times, and it continues to move me to my core. But with this parable, Jesus was showing us *how* to respond with mercy.

Here we have an expert in Old Testament law trying to tangle Jesus in a word competition: What is the definition of *neighbour*? But Jesus responds with a story on what mercy looks like.

This good man from the foreign and unpopular region of Samaria was going about his daily business. He happens upon a very real problem that needed someone to respond *well*. A Jewish man has been robbed and left for dead on the side of the road. The other two characters who come along who could have helped had reasons that they turned into excuses for steering away from the problem.

I am sure there have been many occasions when I have responded in ways that took me away from an issue rather than running toward it. Maybe I didn't want to get involved. Maybe I had no idea what to do. Maybe I was feeling unqualified to bring help. But Jesus is showing us that responding well can be messy, inconvenient, and ... totally the Jesus way.

The question isn't primarily what the definition of *neighbour* is but what *compassion* is. I think Jesus is teaching us that compassion is sympathy for the suffering of others that includes a desire to help.

Can we take it further and say that this is the very nature of Christ in flesh? Throughout the Gospels, you'll see Jesus being moved by compassion. He often stopped what He was doing, turned toward the chaos, and performed a miracle.

Jesus is showing us that responding
well can be messy, inconvenient,
and ... totally the Jesus way.

What is mercy? The dictionary tells us that it's a depth of kindness, an impulse to bring relief and the easing of distress or pain.

James 5 says that the Lord is full of compassion and mercy. Jesus is literally "Mercy on Display." How clearly we see this at the cross!

The cross has made the way for us
So we can come and call upon Your name Jesus
And now oh death, you've lost your sting
As love has triumphed over sin and grave

Part of the beauty of responding well to a need is that we ourselves receive a deep sense of fulfilment that nothing else can bring. It's part of how God has designed us as human beings. "If you pour out that which you sustain your own life for the hungry and satisfy the need of the afflicted, then shall your light rise in the darkness, and your obscurity and gloom become like the noon day" (Isa. 58:10).

We can become so consumed by all of our own needs that we miss hearing the cries of even those who are closest to us. I pray that our hearts will be open to hear and then respond to the things God is asking us to attend to. We cannot respond to everything, and we don't want to get into a theology of works or earning our way to God. It's simply the art of responding to the gentle tug of the Holy Spirit's voice when He whispers, "This one is yours. I am with you. Let's go."

One of the things I love about this Samaritan is that he put the wounded man on his own donkey, secured him, and paid his expenses to ensure the care would continue even in his absence. This was not a quick fix response, but a care-filled, generous-to-the-core, Christ-reflecting response.

There is great power to the thought of being lifted by the Lord: "You are the glory, and the lifter of my head" (Ps. 3:3).

As I have gotten older, I have learned to insert a bit of margin in my everyday, both in time and resources, so that if there is something I need to respond to, I have already created the ability to stop and help. This also sets my course of expectation. It causes me to be more aware, to look around me with eyes that are eager to see need. So often, our lives are so full that we have *no* margin for the real-life encounters that happen in between the organised plannings of our days.

Luke 11:42 is always a great challenge to sit in: "For you tithe mint and rue and all manner of herbs, and yet pass by the justice and the love of God." Ouch. This Scripture is saying that we can do all the right things and almost get into living by the law ... and yet still miss the very people God has put in our lives to impact.

God's mercy on display is seen through the many layers of Jesus' life at work in and through us. This story of the Samaritan gives us a very practical way of loving the stranger, the outcast, the one who has been beaten up by life.

A question to consider today:

Do you have margin in your schedule—and your heart—to respond to a need like the Samaritan did? What is maybe one change you could make in your day-to-day life that would free you up to respond in the way that the Holy Spirit is leading?

Listen to "Yes Again."

Day 29

Yes Again

Many years ago, God brought to my attention the Hebrew word *henini*. It is used in relation to one of the first times we hear the word *worship* in the Bible.

It is first found in Genesis 22, in the story of Abraham and Isaac.

> Sometime later God tested Abraham. He said to him, "Abraham!"
>
> "Here I am," he replied.

As an aside, can I just add here that our English definition gives no hint as to the wholehearted approach to the words "Here I am"? The Hebrew word behind the phrase is *heneni*, which means, "Whatever it is You are about to ask of me, Lord, and *before* You even ask, my answer is yes!"

Then God said, "Take your son, your only son, whom you love—Isaac—and go to the region of Moriah. Sacrifice him there as a burnt offering on a mountain I will show you."

Early the next morning Abraham got up and saddled his donkey. He took with him two of his servants and his son Isaac. When he had cut enough wood for the burnt offering, he set out for the place God had told him about. On the third day Abraham looked up and saw the place in the distance. He said to his servants, "Stay here with the donkey while I and the boy go over there. We will worship and then we will come back to you."

Abraham took the wood for the burnt offering and placed it on his son Isaac, and he himself carried the fire and the knife. As the two of them went on together, Isaac spoke up and said to his father Abraham, "Father?" "Yes, my son?" Abraham replied. "The fire and wood are here," Isaac said, "but where is the lamb for the burnt offering?"

Abraham answered, "God himself will provide the lamb for the burnt offering, my son." And the two of them went on together.

When they reached the place God had told him about, Abraham built an altar there and arranged

the wood on it. He bound his son Isaac and laid him
on the altar, on top of the wood.

Then he reached out his hand and took the knife
to slay his son. (vv. 1–10)

We know what happens next: God brings a ram for a sacrifice, spares Abraham's son, and says, "Because you have done this and have not withheld your son, your only son, I will surely bless you" (vv. 16b–17a).

This word *henini* rattled my world for many years, causing Mark and I to look at what we had actually said yes to, and asking if this kind of pre-existing yes to God was what the Lord was requiring. It was exciting and hard at the same time. After all, to say *yes* to something means you will have to say *no* to something else.

All these years later, post-COVID, after some family health challenges, losing our sister-in-law to a long and brave battle with cancer, and experiencing heartbreaking betrayal, I could sense the Holy Spirit asking me to walk away from some of the deep pain and to say, "Yes Again" to His calling.

To be completely honest, I didn't say yes right away, as I would love to tell you I did. I wrestled with my *yes*. What was this going to require of me and my family? Saying yes does not mean what follows will be easy. However, there is something wonderful that accompanies obedience to the Lord. Though it may be hard, it assures us that the rewards are deep and wide.

During this season of wrestling, I had the joy of being with three of my dear friends: Lindy Coffer, Mitch Wong, and Dustin Smith. These are the most wonderful humans, genuine worshippers, and crazy-great songwriters. There they sat, around my kitchen table, and we started talking about the call of God on our lives. It wasn't long before we agreed that saying yes *continually* was required to live our lives of obedience before God.

When it came to putting this chorus together, a line just came out of my mouth: "Whether I live or whether I die, Oh let it be for Christ. Whether I live, whether I die, Your name be glorified." Here's the full chorus:

> *Whether I live, whether I die*
> *I'll let it be for Christ*
> *Whether I live, whether I die*
> *Your name be glorified*
> *Jesus I give all of my life*
> *A living sacrifice*
> *I say yes again*
> *I say yes again*

I realise that these words will be hard for some to sing—and to mean them. It took me a little while too. But I pray they inspire you to take some time to have a conversation with God about going deeper with Him, to whisper your *hineni*, and then leave the rest to Him.

I read a study recently that revealed over 350 million Christians suffer high levels of persecution and discrimination for their faith every year. In this turbulent world we live in, with much of the world at war or in threat of war, and with millions of Christians sitting in countries where they live in literal life-or-death persecution daily, saying yes to the purposes of God doesn't mean saying yes to ease or comfort. It means that you will do your best to follow the promptings of the Holy Spirit no matter what.

I don't think any of us who live in the relatively safe West have any real idea of how tough life can be for most of the world. A friend sent me a photo recently of persecuted women in Afghanistan. As I read about the rules against these precious women becoming even more intense than they are already, it made me weep. Yet there are believers who live amongst these women daily, showing them Christ through their sacrificial yes, and displaying the radical love of God through their daily devotion to the cause of Christ. They face daily death threats and daily commands to leave the country God has sent them to, yet they just bravely stay and trust God that where He has led them, He will protect them. Yet a bit like Shadrach, Meshach, and Abednego, that internal resolve of "and even if He doesn't deliver us, we will not bow down to a counterfeit God."

Jesus' life was lived in service. His death on a cross was in service.

In fact, it's this life of lifting others to a life of wholeness, from death to life that is so foundational to salvation through Jesus.

Jesus said, "I am the resurrection and the life. He who believes in Me, though he may die, he shall live. And whoever lives and believes in Me shall never die" (John 11:25–26).

We may never be asked to serve Jesus in war zones (although we may), and we may never be asked to literally lay down our lives for the gospel's sake (although we may), but we are all asked to lay down our lives in one way or another. We are asked every day to forgive others, to pray for our enemies, to pray without ceasing, to love those who have mistreated us. I could go on.

> Through the power of the cross we can
> have confident hope that life—in all its
> fullness—is still the promise of God.

But in saying *yes* to the things we may never understand ... this is where our faith life begins as we continually put our trust in God. When we open our lives up to Jesus, we discover fulfilment like never before. When we begin to live fuelled by love and purposed by God, we discover a love better than life, a love that will not let us go. It is a love that requires us to choose calling over comfort.

How does this verse sit with you: "To me, to live is Christ [He is my source of joy, my reason to live] and to die is gain [for I will be with Him in eternity]" (Phil. 1:21 AMP)?

Maybe you are like me and have to continually wrestle with this thought of an intentional *yes* and yielding to God. But let me encourage you that through the power of the cross we can have confident hope that life—in all its fullness—is still the promise of God, and no matter where we find ourselves, God is still on the throne and still in control.

Lord, I say *yes* again.

Listen to "I Am Yours."

Day 30

I Am Yours

It's day thirty of our *Testament* devotional journey. I pray that this season together has deepened your faith in God and helped you to remember all the stories of God's faithfulness in your own life. Your testament is Jesus and His finished work in and through your life.

Consider these words of Jesus, in which we see a revelation of our worth to God Himself:

> Look at the birds of the air; they do not sow or reap or store away in barns, and yet your heavenly Father feeds them. Are you not much more valuable than they? ... Are not two sparrows sold for a penny? Yet not one of them will fall to the ground outside your Father's care. And even the very hairs of your head are all numbered. So don't be afraid; you are worth more than many sparrows. (Matt. 6:26; 10:29–31)

These words just make my heart so happy.

Sparrows are everywhere. They were cheap food back in Jesus' day. We read here that the Father cares so deeply for His people that even the hairs on our heads are numbered. And if God Himself knows every time a single sparrow falls to the ground, how much more does He love and care for each of His children?

One of my favourite songs is "His Eye Is on the Sparrow." It expresses this concept so beautifully.

> Why should I feel discouraged
> Why should the shadows come
> Why should my heart be lonely
> And long for heaven, heaven and home
> When, when Jesus is my portion
> My constant friend is He
> Oh, oh oh, His eye is on the sparrow
> And I know He watched, watched it over me
> I sing because I'm happy (happy)
> I sing because I'm free (free, free, free)
> For His eye, His eye is on the sparrow
> And I know, I know He watches over me[14]

These lyrics were written by Civilla Martin, who shares her own journey of this revelation:

Early in the spring of 1905, my husband and I were in Elmira, New York. We formed a deep friendship with a couple by the name of Mr and Mrs Doolittle—true saints of God. Mrs Doolittle had been bedridden for twenty years. Her husband was an incurable cripple who had to propel himself to and from his business in a wheelchair. Despite their afflictions, they lived happy and fulfilled Christian lives, bringing inspiration and comfort to all who knew them. One day while we were visiting with the Doolittles, my husband commented on their bright hopefulness and asked them for the secret of it. Mrs Doolittle's reply was simple: 'His eye is on the sparrow, and I know He watches me.' The beauty of this simple expression of boundless faith gripped the hearts and fired the imagination of Dr Martin and me. The hymn 'His Eye Is on the Sparrow' was the outcome of that experience.

Despite hardship and pain, the Doolittles continued to shine the light and love of Jesus, knowing their worth *in* Christ and *to* Christ.

I wonder, could the same be said of my life? How about you?

When I was fifteen, I first heard about the good news of Jesus' forgiveness, salvation, and peace. At that moment, my heart, which had been searching for *home*, finally found what it was looking for. From then till now, I have confidently declared "I am Yours" to my Saviour.

God of peace, God of strength
God of wonders, My defence
I will worship at Your throne
Your sacrifice has made me whole
I am Yours
I am Yours

I am so thankful that God didn't just see me in my sin and leave me there, but He saw me and loved me as His child. Our God is not far off, aloof and unconcerned. He is here with us, to be experienced. He welcomes us to speak with Him as a friend, and He speaks to us as we draw near to Him. This is the beauty and power of our God: Though He holds the whole world in His hands, He also comes close and assures you that He holds *your* world in His hands.

There are so many chapters in God's Word that really are eerily similar to the world we live in today. In Isaiah 45, for example, we see that the nations surrounding Israel were fashioning idols to worship (much like our world right now, idolising so many created things rather than worshipping the One who created it all). God encourages these nations to exchange the idols they can carry in their hands for the worship of Him, a God who will carry them in His hands: "Turn

to Me and be saved, all you ends of the earth; for I am God, and there
is no other" (v. 22).

> God welcomes us to speak with
> Him as a friend, and He speaks to
> us as we draw near to Him.

As this world gets darker and you experience this life and its
groaning, you are going to have to reconcile *who* God is, *who* you are,
and *what* your life is all about.

Jesus said, "Follow Me" many times in the Gospels. He used
these two simple words to call Peter, Andrew, James, and John as His
disciples:

> As Jesus was walking beside the Sea of Galilee, he
> saw two brothers, Simon called Peter and his brother
> Andrew. They were casting a net into the lake, for
> they were fishermen. "Come, follow me, Jesus said,
> and I will send you out to fish for people." At once
> they left their nets and followed him.
>
> Going on from there, he saw two other broth-
> ers, James son of Zebedee and his brother John. They
> were in a boat with their father Zebedee, preparing

their nets. Jesus called them, and immediately they
left the boat and their father and followed him.
(Matt. 4:18–22)

God doesn't ask us to follow Him casually, as if He's merely a
lifestyle choice. In fact, following Jesus, living with that "I am Yours"
declaration, can be a really difficult life, especially in the days we are
living in now, when faith in Jesus is sometimes seen as mean and
narrow-minded. But God asks us to turn from living life our way and
turn to living life His way. To love God and others with a miraculous
love that will truly heal you from the inside out. Living with a love that
is a noticeable *testament* to those around us.

He promises eternal life, joy unspeakable, even in the midst of
unthinkable darkness. He promises we can walk *through* the problems
securely in Him.

May I ask you right now to consider your life in the light of God's
great love for you? Take a moment to think about the price Jesus willingly and lovingly paid for you. Let's pray to commit our hearts and
lives to the glory of God. Today, He says, "Follow Me." Today, let's you
and I again say *yes*.

Dearest Lord Jesus, today I am so very aware of my
continued need for You. With all my heart I say *yes* to
following You. I turn away from living life my own
way and ask that You will lead me and speak to me

as I live my life Your way. Fill me with Your Spirit, thank You for loving me, and thank You for the promise of life with You today and forever. Amen.

If you have prayed that prayer sincerely today, may I encourage you to find yourself a good local church in your area, and just jump on in. Begin to grow in the things of God. Ask if they have a good Bible study in your area that you can join. It's knowing the Word of God deep in your soul that feeds and grows your walk with Jesus.

Thank you for being on this journey of God's faithfulness with me. May His love continue to shape and mould you as you reflect His nature to those around you.

For all of my life, I belong to the Lord. My Testament is Jesus, always and forever.

Much, much love,
Darlene Z

Notes

1. The Methodist Service Book, Methodist Publishing House, 1975, D10, John Wesley.

2. Direct quote.

3. *The Complete Works of C. H. Spurgeon*, vol. 28 (Harrington, DE: Delmarva Publications).

4. *Spurgeon on the Psalms: Book Two*, Bridge-Logos Foundation (2015).

5. First published in 1867.

6. C. S. Lewis, *The Weight of Glory*, Goodreads, accessed November 8, 2024, www.goodreads.com/work/quotes/1629232.

7. C. S. Lewis, *Yours, Jack* (New York: HarperCollins, 2008), 344.

8. A. W. Tozer, *The Pursuit of God* (Chicago: Moody, 2015).

9. Max Lucado, *Unshakable Hope: Building Our Lives on the Promises of God*, Goodreads, accessed November 8, 2024, www.goodreads.com/work/quotes/58318434-unshakable-hope-building-our-lives-on-the-promises-of-god.

10. From the Tyndale commentaries, on the meaning of mercy.

11. *No Compromise: The Life Story of Keith Green* by Melody Green and David Hazard (1989, 2008).

12. Charles Spurgeon, LibQuotes, accessed November 8, 2024, https://libquotes.com/charles-spurgeon/quote/lbq7r6d.

13. C. S. Lewis, Apprenticeship to Jesus, accessed November 8, 2024, https://apprenticeshiptojesus.wordpress.com/2015/06/14/c-s-lewis-quotes/.

14. Hymn composed by Charles Gabriel and C. D. Martin (1905).

Bible Credits